NICK THE GREEK

BY CY RICE

Man with a Racket
Errol and Me
Cleopatra in Mink
Defender of the Damned
One for the Book of Sports
Every Diamond Doesn't Sparkle
My Eyes Are in My Heart
Inside the Dodgers
Get Me Gladys!
Children in Danger
Winning at Gin

NICK ⌘ THE ⌘ GREEK

King of the Gamblers

CY RICE

Funk & Wagnalls   New York

To Las Vegas, the city Nick loved
with all his heart

Preface

I HAD mentioned to sources who wished to remain anonymous that I thought the life story of Nick the Greek would be a fascinating one. They unanimously agreed, but added, "You'll never get it." I asked why. They cited many reasons: Nick shuns publicity; avoids being photographed; won't betray confidences; will never sign his name to any agreement; refuses to permit his voice to be taped.

I wasn't easily dissuaded. I asked them to give me a contact. They were reluctant. Finally they suggested I see Sonny Barry.

Sonny Barry is a ruggedly constructed individual of medium height. Thousands are cut from the same cloth. There are no reasons to give him a second glance—that is, unless you happen to hear him speak.

His is not an ordinary voice. Sounds rumble gutturally from his throat like a mini-earthquake. The vibrational energy occasioning such disturbances can be instantly detonated by reference to the name Nick the Greek. Then a mere "Yes" or "No" becomes a thunderclap. Sonny Barry seemed to possess all of Damon Runyon's characters' tonal qualities blended into a single larynx.

I enlisted his help. He gave the matter careful consideration, and believed the results could be positive. He would plant the seeds in Nick's mind, and if they began to sprout, he would telephone me. A week later Mr. Barry introduced me to Nicholas Andrea Dandolos in the Beverly Hills office of Caesar's Palace, Las Vegas.

Nick was immaculately dressed, his silver-streaked hair neatly groomed. With his figure erect and shoulders squared, it was difficult to believe that this man—often given the sobriquet "The Last of the Gentlemen Gamblers"—was nearing his mid-eighties.

"A hundred writers have been after my story," he recalled. "Why do you think you've got a chance of getting it?"

I said, "The odds aren't impossible. I've heard of 100-to-1 longshots coming in."

His eyes widened. "You a gambler?"

"No, just a writer who wants to do an honest account of your life."

He said, "That would take much paper."

"I've got plenty."

He said, "And it would take a lot of time."

"I've got a lot of time."

He stopped talking, and I could tell he was examining me. I said nothing. Waited. His breathing was labored. Clearing his throat, he said hesitatingly, "I . . . I'm getting old and I guess a lot of people want to know."

I agreed that they did.

For a full minute he didn't speak, as he seemed to be arriving at some decision in his mind. Finally he said, "Come to my hotel tomorrow night at eight o'clock and we'll begin."

The Beverly Crest Hotel in Beverly Hills is a small, smart type of operation catering to Eastern tourists and the local luncheon and dinner trade. It has an intimate swimming pool, a cool, shaded patio, and a popular cocktail lounge.

Errol Flynn stayed here a few weeks prior to his death. Now the hotel boasted of another celebrity: Nicholas Andrea Dandolos, retired gambler, occupying a single room that housed a few personal belongings. Nick had always been a loner who traveled light.

I entered his room carrying my equipment, which consisted of pens, writing pads, tape recorder, and extra tapes. He looked at the recorder, grimaced, and growled, "That thing is out."

"But, Nick," I pleaded, "I don't know shorthand."

He countered, "Somerset Maugham wrote in longhand."

Then I proceeded to argue and gently placate his fears of the recorder. I had a pretty good idea of what they were. "Nick," I said, "I know millions of dollars have gone through your hands, and most of it was undeclared in income tax."

He admitted that was true.

I continued: "Forget the Internal Revenue Service. They've got some heart. They're not going to throw an—an. . . ."

"Old man into jail," he finished the words I was trying to avoid.

Suddenly his breathing became harsh and he reached toward a green painted oxygen tank near his chair, adjusted the nose cone to his face, and turned a valve. I heard the hiss of air.

After about three minutes he removed the nose cone, shut off the cylinder. He must have been reading my mind because he said, "I know exactly what you're thinking. I'll lay you 6 to 5 we get the story finished before I die."

I told him I'd take the bet.

A month passed—a month of steady work crammed with interviews that brought the life of Nick the Greek from its inception on the island of Crete to the present. I closed the lid on the recorder.

"Finished," I said, wearily.

His voice was weak. "Not quite."

I knew what he meant. I pulled out five dollars, handed it to him. The King of Gamblers had won the final bet he was to make.

A week later I paid him a social visit. Repeated knocks on the door brought no response. The door was locked. I located the manager, Gary Mozzochi, and the two of us returned to the room. The manager used a duplicate key and we pushed in.

The room was cold. Breezes were sweeping into it from a wide-open window. It was rather dark; only a patch of moonlight faintly illuminated a small portion of the carpeting. But it was enough to spotlight Nick stretched out naked upon the floor.

I clicked the light switch. We lifted him onto the bed and pulled the covers around him. Dead weight is very heavy. I gasped, "Nick, can you hear me?"

His lips moved tremblingly and I bent my head close to them. Only silence. But then he squeezed my hand. His fingers felt dry and clawlike. I mumbled a lot of assurances I knew were untrue, trying to buoy his spirits. "You're going to be fine, Nick, just fine." The words sounded hollow and hopeless.

The manager telephoned Nick's physician, who in turn summoned an ambulance. The patient was transported to Mt. Sinai Hospital and placed in the Intensive Care Unit.

He died two weeks later, on Christmas Day, 1966.

Nick the Greek—born Nicholas Andrea Dandolos—was a physical phenomenon the like of which the world may not see again. He was a paragon of endurance in games unlisted on Olympic agendas—namely, poker and dice.

It is unlikely that such superb athletes as Joe Namath, Sandy Koufax, or Bill Russell, just to name a random trio, could tolerate Nick's cyclonic pace of days and nights of unabated mental action, *sans* sleep and food. Any athlete's central nervous system would shatter faster psychologically.

In contesting the nonpareils of the sports world, Nick might have been bested in muscular activity, but never in endurance. Attempting to emulate him, athletes would undoubtedly fall asleep on the tables after twenty-four straight hours of gambling. The stress and strain imposed here is more grueling than direct participation in any individual or team sport.

The effect on Nick was negligible. The reasons were axiomatic. He spent a lifetime in training and self-discipline, abiding by his rules, always in peak condition. The result was less emotional reaction to pressures.

To medical science Nick must have been one of the Wonders of the World. On a number of occasions doctors had opportunities to take his blood pressure and listen to his heart after grueling and protracted gambling sessions. Out of curiosity in several instances they even measured his pulse rate while he was in the process of losing many thousands of dollars at Las Vegas dice tables.

His heart rate remained unchanged.

His blood pressure was unchanged.

It was questionable, they agreed, that his electrocardiogram would have indicated any change.

A Las Vegas physician summed Nick up as follows: "He appeared to have an extraordinary ability to withstand emotional shock. He did not display the wide fluctuations in central nervous system reactions that most persons do under such stress."

Nick learned many decades ago that when he consumed too much food his mental acuity diminished. Consequently, if he was gambling for a prolonged period, he deliberately made it a point to avoid overeating. This, he believed, gave him an edge over the competition, to help swing the odds in his favor.

He mentioned, "I know the brain gets more blood supply as a result of fasting because it isn't competing with the process of digestion." He added, "Which is why every man in a breadline is cunningly alert."

Throughout a lifetime of snake eyes, box cars, sevens,

elevens, of points made and crapouts, of pairs, full houses, even royal flushes, of bluffs that failed and bluffs that swept in the pots, Nick sat implacably inscrutable, an expensive cigar held lightly in his mouth.

He was fearful of nothing. Not even death. He was a confirmed fatalist.

His mind was brilliantly sharp, a master of calculation, with photographic retention of the printed word.

I once remarked, "Nick, you're a stoic."

He smiled, and delved into the philosophy he so dearly loved. "A stoic," he informed, "was a member of the school of philosophy founded by Zeno about 308 B.C. The Stoics taught that the wise man should be free from passion, unsubdued by joy or grief, willingly submissive to natural law."

"Well, isn't that *you* in gambling," I said, "unaffected by perturbation, pleasure, pain?"

He nodded.

One of his habits was not carrying a watch. He stated, "You can't gamble by the clock." And that was one reason he loved Las Vegas: time means little there; figuratively speaking, it is a city without clocks. Yet it was astonishing that when anyone asked Nick what time it was, he was rarely off more than a few minutes. He met appointments on time and, incidentally, was a man who liked punctuality in himself as well as others. He despised tardy people.

Although Nick gambled with members of the underworld, he was never actually hoodlum-oriented, or even remotely interested in gangland. Many professional gamblers harbored resentment toward him because he repeatedly refused to socialize with them. His reasons were simple: He didn't speak their language, they didn't speak his. They had only gambling in common. He actually found them objectionable companions, labeling them dull, uninteresting, boring. From the moment he finished his games of chance with unsavory characters, he detached himself, drifting away into another world

—often an academic one where he could freely discuss his beloved philosophy. His wide circle of friends ranged from college professors to social celebrities.

In his span of life, Nick had three loves:

1. Gambling.
2. Philosophy.
3. Women.

Women were a poor third. Often he entered Las Vegas casinos with a beauty on each arm. But they were merely window dressing. Handing each of them four or five hundred dollars, Nick would say, "Enjoy yourselves. I'll see you later."

They would drift away toward the cocktail bar, the slot machines, the dice tables, the roulette wheels, fading into the crowds. Chances were they didn't see their benefactor again that evening. "Later" in Nick's vocabulary was a word of immense latitude that could stretch into a full week.

Nick possessed a high-caliber sense of propriety and was governed by a code of honor. He constantly deplored the breakdown in ethics and morality of anyone. He hated with frightening fierceness anybody who broke his word. In many respects he was an idealist. He deplored society's engrossment with materialistic objectives.

He was not devoted to the pursuit of wealth.

CY RICE
Los Angeles, California

Contents

Preface   vii

I, the American   3

You Can't Cheat an Honest Greek   23

Nick and Lou and Mary Garden   31

The Millionaire   42

Gambling Man   70

A Present from Al Capone   88

Ready for Rothstein   103

A Visit to the Promised Land   118

Operation Bounceback   127

Anyone for Poker?   139

Long Live the King!   160

The Battered Suitcase   177

Las Vegas   193

The Final Years   218

Soon fades the spell, soon comes the night;
Say will it not be then the same,
Whether we played the black or white,
Whether we lost or won the game?

Sermon in a Churchyard
Thomas Babington Macaulay
(1800–1859)

NICK THE GREEK

I, the American

"RAISE your right hand and repeat after me," the clerk instructed.

The year was 1902; the place, the Immigration Department; the city, Chicago.

Up went the hands of twenty-six males with similar ambition: to take this final step, the Oath of Allegiance, and become naturalized American citizens, numerical additions to the nation's burgeoning population of seventy-six million.

The hands represented a medley of nationalities: Scandinavians, Poles, Germans, Italians, Irish, two Englishmen, and a six-foot, dark-haired, swarthy-complexioned Greek who stood at military attention, eyes trained on the Stars and Stripes hanging limply in the hot, stuffy room.

The lone Greek was Nicholas Andrea Dandolos, born in the village of Rethímnon on the island of Crete. He was listening with rapt attention to the voice of the clerk—tired, bored, jaded from countless daily repetitions during his tenure in office—droning the oath. But to the eighteen-year-old Greek youth the words had a special connotation, the importance of each completely obscuring the monotony of the delivery. Years later, when he reminisced on this nameless, faceless public servant, the man who was to become the world's most famous gambler recalled, "The clerk's oratorical powers rose sharply until they seemed to rank with a quartet of spellbinders I was privileged to know: William Jennings Bryan, Billy Sunday, Billy Graham, and Adlai Stevenson."

". . . so help me God," the clerk concluded.

Nick dropped his hand. His face lost its solemnness, brightening as a prideful feeling surged through him. Only yesterday he had crossed Halsted Street to wander away from the section known as Blue Island, the largest Greek settlement in the United States. He had been peering into shop windows, soaking up Americana: the drugstores with their large glass ornamental receptacles filled with colored liquid squatting in front of a light; the barber shop shelves against the walls holding fancy shaving cups owned by customers and bearing their names or initials.

As he strolled down the street, his eyes beholding the sights and his nostrils inhaling the odors of the bustling city, a life-sized wooden Indian loomed in front of a cigar store. Nick stepped backward to admire the ferocity of the redskin.

That was when it happened:

His heel ground hard on the instep of a muscular-looking fellow. The man, fists clenched, and apparently a veteran of street combat, spread his feet to assume a fighter's stance and snarled, "Watch where yer goin', you goddamned Greek!"

Nick apologized in broken English. The slur on his nationality stung. But that was yesterday. No such insults would occur in the future, he naïvely thought, relieved. Now if anyone got mad at him they'd have to call him a "goddamned American!" He could take *that* without injured dignity. The word American was meaningful. Important. They could call him anything, he mused. It didn't matter, really. But they better not forget to add American.

"I, Nick the American," ran through his mind. It had a pleasing ring.

Nick trotted down two flights of stairs, left the building, bought a copy of the Chicago American, a Hearst newspaper, sauntered to a park bench, and sat down to relax and enjoy life in a democracy. Plato's words came to mind: "Democracy, which is a charming form of government, full of variety and disorder, and dispensing a sort of equality to equals and unequals alike."

He liked this interpretation.

He leafed through the pages. To him, poring over an American newspaper was a speedier English lesson than a textbook. He read:

"Chicago is still the best Klondike. [The excitement over the Klondike gold rush in Alaska was at its height.] Today there live in Chicago over 200 men whose fortunes reach and pass the million mark. Every large fortune was made here. What you need is an outfit of good sense, sobriety, industry, economy, and stick-to-it-iveness. Without an exception, so far as can be ascertained, these millionaires started in without capital."

The article further related that one of the millionaires, Silas B. Cobb, who had arrived in Chicago without enough money to pay his fare to the captain of the schooner bringing him in, became a model citizen, "never kept a clerk or a bookkeeper, never asked any man to go on his note, never went to law in his life, never paid a lawyer or a doctor a cent," and had amassed fifteen million dollars.

The feature writer went on to list the leading millionaires of the city, and some of the names were familiar to Nick: Marshall Field, Potter Palmer, Philip D. Armour, Montgomery Ward, William Deering, Cyrus McCormick, Samuel W. Allerton, John and Michael Cudahy, and Gustavus Smith.

Young Nick, although in business, harbored no thoughts or ambitions to join this charmed money circle. His chief interest in life was philosophy—and who ever heard of a wealthy Plato, Socrates, Aristotle?

What amused him most in the article was the mention by Gustavus Smith that "no man is rich enough to smoke twenty-five cent cigars"; and that it was said of Samuel W. Allerton, a packer who once bought up all the hogs in Chicago, that "he could taste a steak and tell from which section of the country it came."

Of more than passing interest to Nick—who was one day to acquire a reputation as a gourmet—was the menu printed in the newspaper of a luncheon eaten by the Chief Executive, President William Harrison. He was intrigued by the robust meal, which included crème de terrapin, sherry solero, fillet of white fish, Roman punch, chicken wings, champagne, larded quail, Château Pichen, cheese and crackers, fruit and cake, and coffee.

Folding the newspaper neatly, he held it in his lap. The air had cooled a little, through the courtesy of the big weather control factor, Lake Michigan, which at the moment was wafting a few breezes toward the grateful citizenry. Maybe tonight, Nick thought happily, he could lie naked under a sheet instead of on top. He noticed a few small birds hopping about, hopeful of a handout or a worm foolhardy enough to surface during this heat wave. Two gray squirrels chased one another up a tree. A park attendant, eyes trained on the sun-bleached grass, came along and speared a discarded candy wrapper on the sharp end of his wooden stick.

Leaning against the hard bench slats, Nick watched a woman approaching. She had a pretty face, and wore the prevailing fashions: a ground-length dress cinched at the waist, a huge straw hat sporting brightly colored imitation fruit. He particularly noticed an absence of figs. Figs were his business. And business was only fair.

As the woman passed the bench, Nick gave a perceptible start, noticing that she bore some resemblance to what Fatma might appear like when she was older. . . .

* * *

He would never forget Fatma. Because of her—the start of a chain of events—he was now an American citizen. He was also lucky to be alive and not decapitated by the sharp, curving blade of a sword wielded by an outraged and cuckolded Turk.

His thoughts regressed, sailing across the Atlantic Ocean, through the Strait of Gibraltar, into the Mediterranean Sea, speeding north over the Sea of Crete to the legendary Aegean, finally reaching the City of Smyrna. Later the name Smyrna was replaced by Izmir. Izmir today is a bustling Turkish city of a million people.

The Dandolos family had moved to Smyrna from Crete. A port on the Gulf of Smyrna, inlet of the Aegean Sea, it was the birthplace of Homer—a poorly lighted, unsanitary city, where small incidents triggered turbulent tempers that often burst into violence. After midnight, unless rescued by police walking vicious trained dogs, a person stood an excellent chance of getting killed—especially if he happened to be a Greek. The Greeks and the Turks had a cat-dog loathing for each other.

Nick had a good friend in the city named Adam. His family, prosperous Greeks, owned a large department store. Adam was nearly four years older than Nick, whose parents kept discouraging the relationship, predicting, "He's too worldly and will get you into trouble, Nicholas."

The trouble that would engulf Nick was no fault of Adam's.

Many of the wealthy Turks in Smyrna had harems. On Saturday afternoons the harem girls, under the surveillance of eunuchs, went shopping. Adam and Nick stood around the store in the role of girl-watchers—a pleasurable yet unrewarding pastime. Nick yearned to go a step further.

He persuaded Adam to converse with one of the eunuchs

and occupy his attention by displaying some merchandise in another part of the store while he would attempt small talk with a particular girl. He spoke Turkish fluently.

Adam was apprehensive. "Be careful, Nick," he warned, reminding, "she's someone else's property, you know."

Nick shrugged off the advice. It was a challenge, and youth is quick to accept one, regardless of danger. When he saw Adam leading the eunuch to a distant counter, he accosted the girl and politely whispered flattery into her ear. She was examining hosiery. Very slowly she turned toward him. Her face was completely covered by the traditional veil.

After first glancing cautiously about, the girl divulged softly, "My name is Fatma," and in an undertone cautioned, "It is very risky for you to speak to me."

"The brave deserve the lovely," Nick said gallantly.

She laughed lightly. "But you know nothing of my looks."

"Some day," Nick began, "I hope to see your face, and then . . ."

He heard a sharp whistle from Adam, a danger signal previously agreed upon, meaning that the eunuch was approaching.

"Next week," he said to her hurriedly, merging with the crowd of shoppers.

Most of that night he tossed and turned restlessly, unable to sleep, Fatma consuming his thoughts. He considered her age, guessing at sixteen, which was to prove accurate.

The following week he saw her again, and on this occasion gave her a present: a lace handkerchief a friend of his mother's had sent her from Brussels. Fatma was very grateful, thanking Nick repeatedly.

He was to bestow many costly gifts on women throughout his life, but none was ever received with such a genuine show of appreciation as was this simple, inexpensive one.

Almost fifteen years after giving Fatma the handkerchief, he felt sorry for a Broadway chorus girl he occasionally dated, who would come out of the theater exit in midwinter, the icy wind whipping into her cheap, thin cloth coat as snowflakes swirled around her head.

Handing her a thousand dollar bill, Nick bowed slightly, advising, "Go buy yourself a nice warm fur coat, my dear."

She had been shivering, but now she stopped, indignant and angry. Her voice rose sharply as she screamed, "You cheap phony, playing a joke on me!"

With that, she tore the bill into shreds, tossing the pieces into the air, the wind scattering them among the crowds in Times Square. The next night a girl friend, who had witnessed the brief drama and knew Nick and his reputation, broke the news to her. "That was real money you had in your hand, honey. Nick the Greek never plays practical jokes."

Some speculate that eventually the girl recovered from the shock.

Nick continued seeing Fatma each week—same time, same eunuch, but a different place: a mosque, which was considered a safer rendezvous. By this time he had struck up a friendship with the eunuch and, aided by a few handfuls of piasters, charmed him over to his side.

Then, on a day when Fatma and Nick could hear gentle raindrops falling on the mosque roof, she reached for his hand, leading him to a dim archway. "Now," she said, "look quickly."

The veil was lifted, instantly dropped back in place. It was only a split-second glimpse, but it was enough to drive the youth nearly mad, far more stimulating than the bodies of a parade of ladies of easy virtue who would in the future consider it an honor to disrobe before the famed gambler.

"No man has seen my face," Fatma whispered, adding, "and no man has touched my body."

She mentioned the name of the Turk, a powerful politician,

within whose seraglio she lived. "I threatened him with a knife and he has let me alone."

Before Nick had a chance to comment, Fatma said, "Nicholas, you come to me tonight. My eunuch will bring you."

An arrangement was made. Nick went home, bathed, and shaved carefully with his father's razor because it was sharper than his. He met the eunuch, who led him through a maze of dark, twisting streets. He was barely aware of making that initial trip. His feet seemed wrapped in drifting clouds. Anticipation was strong. And sweet. Very sweet.

Fourteen harem girls were housed on the first floor of a building—sort of a women's barracks. It was situated in the center of a flower garden alongside a cemetery. Mohammedans considered a harem a sacred place, forbidden to infidels.

Fatma's eunuch nudged him, pointing. "The open window. Go on through. Quietly."

Nick carefully, noiselessly climbed in. Once inside, his senses swam dizzily from the sight of her. No veil covered the soft beauty of her smooth-skinned, oval-shaped face, the deep blue eyes, the tiny tilt of her nose. She wore something blue and light and billowy and trailing, made from the purest Damascus silk.

"Hello, Nicholas," Fatma greeted in a voice that sounded as if she had swallowed the stars.

Food was beautifully arranged on a small table whose surface was composed of rectangular pieces of inlaid ivory. There was a Turkish water pipe for him to smoke, and giant pillows to lounge on. He nibbled on a piece of *meze* and puffed on the pipe, which scented the room with an aromatic odor. Fatma removed his shoes and began gently but firmly massaging his feet.

On such an occasion as this, when Nick was absolute monarch, he should have been imbued with social ease and grace. He wasn't. On the contrary, he was extremely nervous. He had never experienced an affair with a woman.

* * *

Nick had a wonderful evening with Fatma. Soon he began visiting her every other night. The third visit was the most important. It was then that he didn't touch the food or smoke the pipe. That was the evening they consummated their love. Nick strove for restraint—to be patient and understanding—and he believed that he gave the lovely girl great pleasure, possibly ecstasy. Afterward, homeward bound through the dark streets, he felt so exhilarated he wanted to shout victoriously of his entry into manhood.

Several months passed. Nick couldn't seem to satiate himself with Fatma. Then one night trouble reared its Turkish head. Soon after he crawled through the window there was a frantic tapping on the door, and the frightened voice of the eunuch was heard imploring, "Run, boy! Go out fast!"

Nick listened, and from down the long corridor came the sound of heavy approaching footsteps. The Turk, he correctly guessed, must have been tipped off. Nick had never seen him personally—only his picture in the newspapers, captioned "Powerful Politician."

The majority of Turks could skillfully wield swords. Greek history books have graphically described the results of their carnage. Nick had no intention of allowing history to repeat itself.

He heard the Turk bellowing, "Where is that black soul of a Greek that I'll cut to ribbons!"

Fortunately, he had just finished dressing. He turned toward Fatma. Her face was lined with worry. She suggested, "Hide in the closet!"

He rejected the idea. The closet was too obvious. His place of entrance seemed the logical exit. Throwing open the window, he jumped, streaked through the garden, hurdling the low cemetery wall for a shortcut.

It was only when he stubbed a toe on a tombstone that he realized his shoes were still in Fatma's quarters.

The burial grounds were capacious and pine-tree-studded. The night was windy, and sporadic gusts blowing through the treetops produced a series of high-pitched whispers similar to ghostly voices, adding to the eerie atmosphere.

The fleeing young man realized the front gates would be locked, with probably a watchman on duty, and that in order to escape he must scale the cemetery wall. This presented a problem. Composed of crumbling brick, the wall at this point was higher than where he had first jumped it. Breathing hard, he approached the barrier and stood motionless to study the obstacle. He was speculating on running and taking a mighty leap, in the hope that his hand might grasp the top and drag his body up and over.

It was a moment of decision. Perhaps a trained athlete could make it. But a student of philosophy . . . ?

Then he heard voices on the other side. He stood stock still, trying to quiet his labored breathing. One of the voices ordered distinctly, "Throw him over here."

Something huge, unwieldy, heavy, and pulpy crushed Nick beneath its weight. Momentarily stunned, he was knocked flat on his back with an indescribable something pinning him down. Slowly he squirmed from under whatever was on top of him, and struggled to his feet. His blouse felt wet and sticky.

Bending down, squinting in the dark, he examined the mysterious thing that had come over the wall. It was the body of a human! Just then the moon struggled away from a black cloud and shone down like a spotlight. Below him Nick recognized the unmistakable features of a Turk. He was bloody, disheveled, dirt-stained. Nick guessed he had been stabbed.

Nick could never remember how he scaled the wall, but he attributed it to "strength generated from pure fright." He ran wildly through a maze of streets until he spotted a horse-drawn cab. The driver stared at his blood-caked clothing, but only asked for an address.

Upon reaching home, Nick sneaked up to his room on the top floor of the small house, careful not to wake his parents, slipped into a bathing suit, and after burying his clothes, ran to the ocean, plunged in to battle the inbound breakers, and swam until he felt cleansed.

The next morning he couldn't find a single item in the newspaper about the murdered man who had been flung over the cemetery wall. He went to see Adam at the store. At the door he felt a hand on his shoulder. It was Fatma's eunuch.

"Fatma refused to reveal your name," the eunuch said.

Nick breathed a sigh of relief. It was short-lived. The eunuch said that another eunuch had learned of the clandestine meetings and in order to curry favor had tattled.

"Did he know my name?" Nick asked. A lot depended on the answer—possibly his very life.

No, the eunuch did not know his name. But he had a physical description, and it was only a question of time before the Turk's influence and money would manage to track him down.

Nick asked for advice.

"Leave Smyrna as fast as possible," the eunuch said.

Nick hardly touched his food at the family dinner table that evening. His father and mother, noticing that he was disturbed, suggested that he tell them if anything were wrong. He confessed the entire affair. It was decided to consult with his godfather, George Poulos, a wealthy rug merchant. Mr. Poulos had intended sending him to England for postgraduate study at Oxford University. Plans were changed. The boy who spoke Greek, English, Turkish, and French, plus a smattering of German and Russian, holder of a degree in philosophy from the Greek Evangelical College at Athens, adjudged by his professors "a budding mathematical genius," would embark for America and set up in business: figs.

George Poulos agreed to stand the expense.

Nick wondered how he could apply his educational background to figs—and especially to the pursuit of money, for which he cared little. His uncle thought it was a golden opportunity and assured him that all of America was waiting eagerly to taste the importations of Nicholas Andrea Dandolos.

Now Nick had nothing personal against the fig. In fact, the fig to him was a fascinating fruit: reference to its cultivation was found in the Hebrew Scriptures. (There was another object of ancient civilization that was later to interest him more: dice. Back in the Stone Age, gambling men were throwing numbered cubes made of animal bone.)

"You go study the fig business," his godfather counseled.

Nick asked him, "How long do I have?"

"Two days."

"That's all?"

"You're a smart boy," was the answer. "Two days are enough."

Thus began a forty-eight-hour crash course in figs. According to his godfather, a world traveler, Nick would establish a warehouse in Chicago and supply the Greeks living there who operated restaurants, grocery stores, confectionaries, vegetable markets. The figs would be shipped over in twenty-five- and fifty-pound boxes.

He plunged into deep study. He read books, went to markets. Fig, he learned, was the popular name given to plants of the genus *Ficus*. *Ficus carica* were the figs of commerce indigenous to Asia Minor and Syria, but occurring in wild state in most of the countries bordering the Mediterranean.

At dinner the night before he was to leave Turkey, his father stated, "Nicholas, there are many kinds of figs, and it will take you some time to learn their names and recognize them."

"Yes, Father," Nick agreed, and could not resist rattling off some of his newfound knowledge, reciting: "Agen, Brown Ischia, Brown Turkey, Brunswick, Col di Signora Bianca, Col di Signora Nigra, Early Violet, Bourjassotte Grise, Grosse Marseilles, Negro Largo, White Ischia, White Marseilles . . ."

"Enough," his father interrupted, and addressing his wife, said with pride, "You see, he already knows the business."

Memorizing a few names of figs did not a successful business make, Nick was soon to discover in America. Competition was stifling him. Every Greek he met seemed to be either in the restaurant or fig business.

After a few years in figs he was earning about $12.50 per week, but by penurious living he had saved what to him was a vast sum of money: exactly $250.00. This did not last long once he learned—or thought he learned—the game of poker.

The Greeks of Blue Island were crazy over a dice game called Barbudi. It was practically their national pastime. Nick sometimes played with a friend, Bill Becharus, who ran a small coffee house. He did well, but the game, involving throwing three dice, failed to excite his interest.

One night he kibitzed at an American game—poker—and was truly fascinated. He asked Becharus about it. Becharus tried to explain the game orally, which was a tedious and almost impossible task—especially when the lesson lasted only fifteen minutes.

Equipped with this scant knowledge, Nick wanted to try his luck. Becharus advised him to keep away from professional games where there was a house cut, explaining how this percentage could whittle down a man's chips. He suggested Nick play in a downtown Chicago saloon where there was no house cut, the management making money only on drinks. They had five tables of different limits: a nickel ante, a ten cent, a twenty-five, a fifty, and one for a dollar.

"Start at the nickel-ante game," Becharus counseled.

Nick sat down at the dollar table.

Two hours later he got up minus every cent he had in the world. The next day in the coffee house he saw Becharus.

"How did you do?" Nick was asked.

"Lost two hundred and fifty," was the reply.

Becharus, who knew something of Nick's financial situation, was stunned. "It's your *only* money."

"I'll get it back," Nick said.

"How?" Becharus wanted to know.

Reaching into his coat pocket, Nick pulled out a deck of worn cards. "I will study these—all fifty-two."

Becharus shook his head and sighed audibly. Just another crazy Greek, he speculated. He couldn't personally protect every immigrant. Yet this Greek was a shade different. He seemed unperturbed by his losses, which, relatively speaking, were tremendous. Some people in Nick's shoes, having just been wiped out, might have considered anything from flagellation to suicide. He surely must, Becharus believed, be suffering inside and need cheering up.

"Let me buy you a drink," Becharus proposed.

Nick smiled and read his thoughts. "Thanks, I don't need one."

"But you must feel terrible."

"Quite the contrary," Nick returned. "I am unaffected. And I definitely do not subscribe to the theory of Gustave Flaubert."

Becharus hesitated, then said, "I do not know Mr. Flaubert."

"Mr. Flaubert," Nick stated, "is dead some twenty years. He was a French novelist, an untiring stylist striving for complete objectivity and exactitude of expression. He said, 'Humanity has but one objective: to suffer.' I do not agree with him."

Bidding his friend goodbye, Nick left the coffee house. For a full minute after the door eclipsed his tall, straight figure, Becharus, standing transfixed, stared after him. It was he who needed the drink.

Back in his room Nick began dealing out poker hands on his bed. Hundreds of them. He made notations on a pad. There were no books in those days that provided readers with percentages. He learned what a fool he had been trying to draw a straight in the middle or to raise on a four flush as he had done. At the end of a week he had figured a table of percentages that was similar to those found in instructional books today.

Armed with his newfound knowledge, he returned to the scene of his debacle and sat down in the nickel-ante game. He started with ten dollars' worth of chips, money he had borrowed. In turn, he broke each game, including the dollar table, and at five o'clock in the morning walked out with $750.00.

He learned a great deal that evening—particularly, that there was more to poker than merely luck and understanding percentages. Characteristics were highly important—the individual characteristics of opposing players. A study of faces and mannerisms was often as revealing as the privilege of peering into hands to see the cards his opponents were holding.

He was to become an astute student of physiognomy.

Nick rose from the bench, boarded a streetcar bound for Halsted Street, and entered the Greek section, where he dropped in to see his friend Demetrius and break the news of his naturalization. Demetrius operated a small flower stand. He liked Nick, and every time he saw him, slipped a white carnation into his buttonhole, unconsciously forming a habit that was to continue during social evenings throughout Nick's lifetime.

Demetrius never accepted any money. "Forget it," was his usual answer, and he always concluded with: "When you become a millionaire you can buy me a farm outside of Athens."

This was invariably good for a chuckle and the reply, "If you're depending on the fig business, I don't think you'll ever get your farm."

Demetrius would look up from cutting flower stems, nod his head sagely as if he understood the future, and say, "I've got confidence in you, my boy."

* * *

Never in the wildest stretch of the imagination did the thought cross Nick's mind that within a few years he'd make Demetrius' dream come true. The fig business had nothing to do with it. Hot poker hands did. He left the table one evening with well over $100,000. One quarter of it he gave to a grateful Demetrius—who promptly closed his flower stand and sailed to Athens with his wife. Outside the old city he bought the equivalent of a sprawling western American ranch. Here he spent the rest of his days hunting, fishing, farming, enjoying life to the hilt.

Nick always remembered a paragraph from one of his frequent letters:

After we finish every meal we go upstairs and light the candles in front of a picture of you I had copied life size on the wall and pray for your good health. To us you are a Saint.

In discussing his charitable act, Nick quoted from Aristotle: "Benefactors appear to love in a greater degree those whom they benefit than those who are benefited love their benfactors." However, he didn't believe this bit of philosophy was applicable to the relationship between Demetrius and himself. Their love and admiration, he felt, was mutual.

In his furnished room one of America's newest citizens was living a Spartan existence. His future life was slated to be filled with single hotel rooms—very few suites or penthouses—in New York, New Orleans, Chicago, Las Vegas, Los Angeles, Hot Springs, Louisville, Saratoga, San Francisco—wherever the action might be. A single room was always adequate for his needs.

Although he did maintain a penthouse atop the Beverly Wilshire Hotel in Beverly Hills during World War II, he kept it primarily to provide servicemen returning from combat duty with a place to stay whenever he was out of the city—which was frequently.

He would mature into an uncomplicated man, one who showed little interest in externals. Personal jewelry held no fascination for him, though he derived momentary enjoyment from presenting expensive pieces of it to a variety of women. He had a particular hatred for watches, rarely wearing one.

"Time," he stated, "can place a limitation on pleasure."

It is incidental to a gambler.

In the exciting, fast-moving years ahead his wardrobe would consist of a tuxedo, a full dress suit, and some business clothes supplemented by a few sports coats and slacks—consistently conservative. A man, he often reasoned, could only sleep in one room at a time or wear one suit at a time. He never understood the necessity—or perhaps it was a compulsion—for certain men (his friend George Raft, for example) to possess more wearing apparel than a small clothing store stocked.

Nick climbed the stairs and went into his room. There was a knock on the door. He opened it to admit Chris, a Greek youth about his own age who worked for a grocer. The grocer sometimes bought Nick's figs. They were firm friends. Nick excitedly told him the news of his naturalization.

Chris shook his hand mechanically. "Congratulations," he said unenthusiastically.

"What's the matter?" Nick asked. "Aren't you happy for me?"

"Sure, sure," Chris said rapidly, "only . . ."

"Only what?"

"Well . . ." He hesitated. "You're feelin' good, Nick. Real good. I don't want to spoil your mood. I . . ."

"Come on," Nick urged. "You got something to say, why, say it."

Chris sat down on the only chair. "Remember the poker game you played in last week—a three-handed stud game with a fellow named Louie and one called Jake?" he began.

He certainly did. His luck had been bad. He had lost forty-five dollars of profit from the fig business.

"You were cheated," Chris blurted.

"What!" Nick bounded to his feet from the edge of the bed where he was sitting.

"Yes," Chris repeated emphatically, "cheated."

"But I couldn't be."

"Why couldn't you have been?"

Nick groped for words. "Because . . . because Louie and Jake are . . . are Americans."

Chris didn't understand. "So are seventy-six million others. What's that got to do with it?"

Nick tried to explain, and as he talked, a look of amazement spread over his friend's face at the lack of guile he revealed, his trust and faith in human beings. Bursting with American history he had learned for his citizenship test, he told Chris that this country was a young nation where a person shaped his own destiny to become anything he wanted, from cabbages to kings; that in this land people put their shoulders to the wheel and worked together to build a strong country.

"Nick," Chris said, speaking in Greek, "your reflections are lofty and glorious, but far too unsophisticated. Tell me this: aren't there ever any spoiled figs in your boxes?"

"Some. Why?"

"It's the same with people," Chris said. "A few rotten apples in a barrel, a bad egg in a dozen, the black sheep of a family— so why not a couple of crooked poker players teaming up in a three-handed game to signal each other?"

"But how?"

"By voice, by mannerisms." He raised his shoulders and let them fall. "Many ways are possible."

"They did this to me?"

Chris nodded, and proceeded to unfold the lengthy story of his discovery. Louie and Jake had bragged around Blue Island how they had "taken over the innocent Greek." Chris offered witnesses for proof.

Nick was convinced.

"I'm tired," he said.

"You wish to go to bed?"

"Yes."

Chris left.

Nick made no move to retire. Instead, he paced the floor, his long legs requiring only a few strides to cross the room. He rarely needed a bed; unless shared with a woman to extinguish the flames of passion, this article of furniture was considered merely a place where he could recharge his body with enough vitality so that sleep could be postponed indefinitely.

Chris's revelation left him trembling with suppressed rage. He needed something to calm his nerves, abate his anger. He found an antidote: the philosophy of Euripides, penned before Christ. As he read on and on, his anger melted. And then he finished a stanza that caused him to snap the book shut:

> I think that Fortune watcheth o'er our lives,
> Surer than we. But well said: he who strives
> Will find his gods strive for him equally.

This passage from *Iphigenia in Tauris* was most appealing. Euripides was smarter than Louie and Jake. Yes, Nick mused, he would take the advice of the philosopher and make his gods strive for him.

But how?

He sat in the chair, removed his shoes, leaned back, and rested his feet on the softness of the bed. And he began thinking, slowly constructing a plot with two victims in mind: Louie and Jake.

As the first gray streaks of dawn began filtering through his window, he had it all conceived. It was simple, direct, workable. Every detail dovetailed. Perhaps it was lacking in honesty, but the Greeks believed in "an eye for an eye." He was impatient to begin pulling the strings he would attach to two humans transformed into puppets, to maneuver them by his will.

Revenge, he knew, was a petty victory, impossible to savor properly. It was shallow. Hollow. But, he justified, what he plotted wasn't really revenge in the true sense of the dictionary interpretation: "To inflict harm; to vindicate by avenging." This was a game . . . a game flavored by danger. And the results, if successful, would prove a triumph of ingenuity.

He crossed to the window and peered out. Light was flooding the street and people were beginning to move about. He could hardly wait to start the action.

You Can't Cheat an Honest Greek

T HE preliminary step was to call on his friend, Basil Charuhas, a local theater owner and brother of the infamous "King George," proprietor of a gambling house specializing in Barbudi and various card games.

He outlined his plan.

Charuhas was somewhat less than enthusiastic. "Too dangerous," he commented.

"So is life itself," Nick countered.

Charuhas said resignedly, "I guess you've made up your mind."

"I have."

"Nothing can change it?"

Nick was adamant. "Absolutely nothing."

"Then, if such be the case," Charuhas said, "I'll take you to see my brother."

King George was a stockily built, bushy-eyebrowed archetype of a Greek warrior carrying sword and shield. He had a flowing mustache and, if pondering a problem, his habit was to twist the ends of it. At the moment he was twisting the dark hair strands into temporary curls.

At length, addressing Nick, he gave an opinion. "You are taking a big risk."

"Nick doesn't care," Charuhas spoke up.

Nick nodded in agreement.

"Louie and Jake," King George grinned, "are, I imagine, not of Greek ancestry."

He was assured that if handed a world atlas the pair probably couldn't locate Greece.

"Then I believe the little merchants who sell cards will cooperate," King George said. He asked Nick where the game would be held. Nick said at his room. King George learned the address and promptly drew a map of the Blue Island section, which he knew like the palm of his hand, on a blank piece of paper. Using Nick's street number as a focal point, he did some rapid figuring and came up with an answer.

"Six decks ought to cover the area," he surmised. He motioned Nick and Basil to follow him into his private office. Here there was a small gas stove where King George made and drank daily nearly fifteen cups of a favorite drink of Greeks, coffee. Locating a kettle, he set it atop one of the burners and lit the gas. Steam soon came from the spout.

From a desk drawer he brought forth half a dozen fresh decks of cards. They were all blue-backed.

"Easier on the eyes than red," he mumbled to no one in particular.

Holding each individual package of cards at a distance where it received the full force of the steam, and aided by the corner of a razor blade, he meticulously opened the seals. So gently did he pry them that they were undamaged.

"I hate a cheat," King George muttered venomously.

Then he wiped and dusted a table on which he spread the full deck. He had a bottle of blue ink corresponding to the color of the cards, which were manufactured by one of the legitimate brand-name companies.

Periodically he fired questions at Nick, who was intently watching the proceedings.

"What are you going to play, draw or stud?"

"Stud."

"Good," King George said, inquiring, "how's your eyesight?"

"Perfect."

"And your memory?"

"Retentive."

While he worked painstakingly with a fine-pointed pen, King George discoursed on the methods of marking cards. One popular way, he said, was the "punch" system. A microscopic punch, resembling a thumbtack, could be fastened to a player's forefinger, attached with a tiny piece of adhesive tape. By applying slight pressure, he could press slightly to raise a blister on the back of certain cards. Each time he touched a predetermined spot at one of the corners, he could readily feel it for identification when dealing. "Braille system," King George called it.

Another popular method, he related as he bent low over the spread-out deck, was to use a red or a blue paste. The user hid a dab of one color behind his right ear, the other behind his left. When dealing a hand he could casually scratch his head in a normal manner and transfer the coloring matter onto his thumb, thence to the cards. After an hour of play the shadings would look like ordinary smudges.

"What I'm preparing for you," King George informed Nick, "is the 'reader' system. With it goes a code for you to memorize."

With the touch of an expert, he marked the cards so lightly they were practically undetectable to anyone not equipped with the code. The markings at top and bottom were identical, blending in beautifully with the design on the back of the cards. Only a small part of the card needed to be exposed to the dealer for him to establish recognition.

Nick posed a question to King George. "If I can detect the markings, why can't my opponents?"

King George held up a card for inspection, pointing out, "The design on the back is as confusing as sets of fingerprints. Unless a man knows exactly where to look he can't see any irregularities. It's all in the lines, the dots and the shadings, and they look perfectly normal."

In his work King George used a large magnifying glass and a special indelible ink that would penetrate the wax finish of the cards. It required a steady hand, patience, care, skill. King George was an artist. The color of the shading and the line work had to be done with great exactitude—a perfect mating, not too dark or light.

Nearly finished, King George, prior to making up a code sheet, tested Nick on the shadings of the daisy petals on the backs of the cards. He did remarkably well.

"But there are no shadings on the deuces," he discovered.

"Correct," King George replied, adding, "and for that very reason you will recognize they are deuces."

It took an average of nearly an hour to mark each deck, plus an additional half hour for the code, which Nick carefully folded into his breast pocket.

"I don't know how to thank you enough," he said gratefully.

"Forget it," King George said. "It's for the honor of Blue Island."

Nick said hesitatingly, "Only one more favor."

"Name it."

He wanted to borrow a number of cigar coupons, the kind redeemable for prizes. He left with these and the six marked decks, which King George had carefully replaced in their wrappings, regluing the seals so that it was impossible to detect that the packages had been tampered with.

Nick took a deck to each of the stores that sold cards within easy walking distance of his lodging. Only slight salesmanship was necessary. An outrage had been committed against a Greek, the storekeepers agreed, and they would be willing conspirators in order to wipe the slate clean. Nick accurately described Louie and Jake. Most of the card sellers knew them.

All the money Nick had to his name was a twenty and a five dollar bill. With the twenty dollar bill on the outside, followed by the five and the cigar coupons, which were the same size as legal currency, the padded roll resembled considerable money.

This was his bait.

That night he visited a saloon frequented by Louie and Jake. He located the pair sitting at a table, heads together, talking. Pretending not to see them, Nick passed by.

"Hey, Nick!"

He paused and, swinging his head from side to side, searched the room for the caller.

"Over here, Nick."

He followed the direction of the voice, waved a hand in recognition, and walked to the table.

"Sit down and have a drink," Louie invited.

Nick dropped into a chair and ordered a brandy. When it arrived, Jake tried to pay, but Nick whipped out his bulging bankroll, quickly peeled off the top twenty, and thrust it into the waiter's hand.

The eyes of Louie and Jake bugged.

"You been doing pretty good lately," Jake voiced.

"Figs," Nick said, patting his hip pocket where he had returned the thick roll. "Suddenly business became very good."

Louie laughed lightly. "Glad to hear it," he said. "You deserve some good luck after all the bad luck you had in our card game."

Taking a sip of brandy, Nick said, "They weren't running for me, that's all. Maybe next time. Say!" he exclaimed, hit by a sudden thought. "You gentlemen want to play again?"

They certainly did.

"What about tonight at my place?"

Both men agreed that would be fine.

A time was set. Nick gave his address, finished his brandy, and left. It was unnecessary to turn around upon reaching the door to know what Louie and Jake were doing. He could guess. Undoubtedly they were talking excitedly and laughing and probably using a cliché like, "Once a sucker, always a sucker," followed, perhaps, by the remark, "These dumb foreigners will never learn."

Arrangements for the game were simple. Nick borrowed two camp stools and a drum-style table from a neighbor. The most important was the lighting: it must be good and strong. From the ceiling, so that it descended directly over the drum table, he suspended a powerful light bulb on a long extension cord.

Once again, and for the final time, he studied the King George code, mentally digesting the shadings, dots, and lines. Positive that he had it thoroughly memorized, he tore it into small pieces and threw them into the wastebasket. For a few seconds he stared at the receptacle, then scooped it up and emptied the contents on the table. Separating the shredded paper containing the code, he placed the pieces in an ashtray and burned them. Just in case . . .

The stage was now set. All he had to do was await the arrival of the other members of the cast of a three-man drama and hope it would play without mishap. A mishap could be costly. Perhaps physically so.

He felt prepared. He had taken a lukewarm bath, afraid that hot water might make him torpid, and had eaten lightly. From a battered bookcase he selected Marcus Aurelius Antonius' "Meditations." Then he removed his shoes, stretched upon the bed, and read. Soon his interest focused on the sentence, "By a tranquil mind I mean nothing else than a mind well ordered."

He hoped this applied to him.

There was a knock on the door and muffled voices. He flung it wide and greeted his guests.

"Very cozy," Louie complimented, looking around. Jake grunted in assent.

Nick motioned toward the camp stools, the lone chair, and table.

"Well, should we get started?"

Before Louie and Jake seated themselves, Nick apologized. "Gentlemen," he said, "I'm very sorry, but I forgot a deck of cards."

Louie threw an already opened red deck on the table. "I brought some," he said, shaking the cards from the cardboard cover, and began idly shuffling.

"I'd like a fresh deck if there's no objection," Nick stated flatly.

Louie stopped shuffling and together with Jake stared at him. Before either could answer, Nick laid a fifty cent piece on the table. "If one of you doesn't mind going out, there's a number of places in this neighborhood selling playing cards."

They both started to rise, but Jake picked up the half dollar and said, "I'll be the errand boy."

"Sorry," Nick said.

"We want everyone to be happy," Jake flung over his shoulder as he left the room.

He returned with a blue deck, tossed it on the table. Louie broke the seal with a long, dirty thumbnail, removed the wrapping, shuffled the cards carefully, and passed them to Nick.

"The host should have the honor of the first deal," he said.

Nick cut the cards once and dealt. It was a limit game. A dollar could be bet unless a pair showed; then two dollars was the maximum. On the last card it was permissible to wager up to five dollars. A four flush beat a pair.

At three in the morning a recess was declared. Louie and Jake had run out of money. Louie went for fresh currency, returning within half an hour. Nick's streak continued. In stud poker the first, or hole, card is face down, and Nick had no trouble identifying its shadings or dots or fine lines.

He had done his homework well.

By seven o'clock the game ended. Nick gathered in the last pot. Both visitors were tapped out. They were tired and irritable. Lack of sleep showed plainly in their faces, manifested by the puffiness and redness around their eyes. Nick appeared fresh and alert. He showed Louie and Jake to the door.

"Sorry, gentlemen," he said.

Emptying his pockets, he counted the winnings: $72.50. That meant he had won back the $45.00 previously lost, plus an additional $27.50. First thing in the morning he would give the $27.50 to a crippled woman down the street whose husband had been laid off work. He wanted nothing he wasn't entitled to, a credo he religiously adhered to until a few years before his death.

Nick and Lou and Mary Garden

R UDYARD Kipling hated Chicago. Characterizing it the "most American" of American cities—an innuendo implying it was the nadir of towns—he claimed he found nothing within its confines but an expression of materialism, and to describe his discoveries, wrote:

> I know thy cunning and the greed
> Thy hard high lust and willful deed
> And all th' glory loves to tell
> Of specious gifts material.

Nick did not agree with Kipling in his general dislike for Chicago. He did, however, in the matter of materialism. Money seemed of paramount importance in a capitalistic society. Such thinking left him disenchanted. Barely on speaking terms with money, he wasn't exactly a comet blazing across the commercial skyway. After half a dozen years he was making slow progress in figs, and to supplement his income began moonlighting in bookkeeping for a few Greek storekeepers, which added $18.00 weekly to his earnings.

In his spare time he frequented the Blue Island coffee houses, searching for intellectual stimulation—emulating Diogenes, the Greek cynic philosopher, looking for a "man" who had the true human virtues. His quest was fruitless. Instead, he found mostly gambling. He would stand, an erect youth with a dark, intense face, close to the tables where swarthy Greeks, eyes dancing excitedly, played the ancient Turkish dice game Barbudi. In this pastime the points 3, 5, 6, and 5–6 win for the shooter; 1, 2, and 4 lose for him. The dice are shaken in, and rolled from, a cup.

Observers could not fail to detect in Nick a certain aloofness and reserve mixed with a friendly quality. He was decidedly not the sort of man who could be thumped on the back in buddy-buddy greeting. There was something about him— perhaps powers of perception and analysis—that caused people to feel, often merely after an introduction and desultory conversation, that he knew them far better than they knew him.

He was a loner then and always—an easy man to meet, a hard man to know. He seemed to be surrounded by a veneer, impenetrable as a ring of steel, that stilled inquisitive tongues, warded off personal questions. When he spoke, his eyes bored into those of listeners, holding them hypnotically captive until his flow of words stopped. Should he fail to command the attention of an audience of one, his right index finger would dart rapierlike to poke at a fleshy target just below the shoulder. Sometimes it inflicted pain.

Night after night, making the rounds of the coffee houses, Nick noticed the exhilaration of the winners in Barbudi, the sadness cloaking the losers. He also witnessed that they played for hours, as if transformed into a state of suspended animation. They were in a self-made and self-sealed vacuum, cut off from the world and its realities, where time itself was arrested. The mysticism of it fascinated him.

A student of humanity, he felt that the answer to most perplexities in the world could be unraveled at public libraries.

Here he went to browse and pour over books that he hoped could accurately point a learned finger at, and explain, the sensations experienced while gambling. He came up practically empty-handed until a young lady librarian in the reference room suggested that he read *The Gambler* by the Russian novelist Fyodor Dostoevsky.

He was delighted by the short novel, and even in his octogenarian years he could quote practically verbatim four paragraphs of the text:

> I went into the casino with a confident expectation and at the same time with an excitement I had never experienced before.
>
> I staked straight off twenty friedrichs d'or on even [roulette] and won, staked again and again won, and went on like that two or three times. I imagine I must have had about four hundred friedrichs d'or in my hands in about five minutes.
>
> At this point I ought to have gone away, but a strange sensation rose up in me, a sort of defiance, a desire to challenge it, to put out my tongue at it.
>
> I laid down the largest stake allowed—four thousand gulden— and lost it. Then, getting hot, I pulled out all I had left, staked it on the same number, and lost again, after which I walked away from the table as though I were stunned. I could not even grasp what had happened to me. I spent the rest of the day sauntering in the park.

Nick always felt that, while this story laid bare the viselike grip gambling had on Dostoevsky himself in the autobiographical account of his misadventures, the author failed to reveal his personal reflections after a losing bout at the gambling tables. He believed the sentence "I spent the rest of the day sauntering in the park" to be inconclusive. What transpired inside the writer's mind? Was the germ of suicide forming? Was it masochism? Paranoia? Any recriminations? Could a man, Nick wondered, after such a debacle simulate the turning of a valve in his mind to flood the brain with abstractions?

Or could new and pleasurable speculations be introduced that could chase memories into swift flight?

Could he, Nick Dandolos, become such a master of his own mind?

Hadn't he done this very thing after his first crushing defeat at poker?

Someday he would really test himself.

Combing the plain wooden bookcases of the library, he found and checked out Plato's *Republic*. Back at his rooming house he started to climb the steep flight of stairs to his quarters when he spied a book lying on one of the steps. He stooped and picked it up, as he did every book that ever came within his reach, and flipped open the cover. It was a copy of Grimm's *Fairy Tales*. The library card in the pocket indicated it was a week overdue. Such a book could belong only to the twelve-year-old daughter of his landlady.

"Penelope!" he called.

A child with coal-black hair and deep, sunken eyes appeared.

Nick held out the book. "Is this yours?"

The child answered in the affirmative.

"It is overdue," Nick said gravely, and went on, "The library is the brain of the city—indeed, of civilization itself. This book is part of that brain and must be returned. If everyone took books and none were returned, that brain would die for lack of nourishment, and from then on people would live in ignorance."

Nick always talked like an adult to children.

He handed her the book. "Take it back; it is overdue."

"And so is your rent, Mr. Dandolos," a voice behind him reminded.

He turned to face his landlady, nodded pleasantly, and pushed past her to start up the stairs. Before he reached the first landing he began reciting, the words floating down to her:

Cast away care, he that loves sorrow,
Lengthens not a day, nor can buy tomorrow;
Money is trash, and he that will spend it,
Let him drink merrily, fortune will send it.

The landlady, puzzled, watched him turn down the hall and disappear. "He's an odd one," she mumbled, tapping her head significantly with a long, soiled forefinger. "I ask him for the rent and he gives me poetry instead."

Through Basil Charuhas Nick met Lou Tellegen, a tall, thin, suave, early-day matinee idol of Greek ancestry who was later to establish himself as a great lover in the movies. In the cinematic world of the future, Tellegen came to be known as the Cave Man and the originator of the Cave Man Embrace. This was performed in a standing position. His right arm would crushingly encircle a cinched waistline while his left hand, fingers spread, descended flatly on top of an elaborate hairdo. The willing but struggling victims of this inescapable wrestler's hold were slowly drawn toward his manly loins and pressed against them. Once the bodies touched, the lips followed suit. It was rib-cracking and spine-tingling. Ladies in the audience gasped and, despite the darkness of the theater, hid their faces behind fans.

Many a maiden dreamed of the handsome Lou Tellegen and wished she could trade places with the oft recipient of the kiss, Geraldine Farrar.

In press interviews and fan magazines Tellegen kept repeating that he would never marry until he reached the age of forty because his art meant more. But it was impossible to place a future date on love and marriage, and Tellegen succumbed to a woman's charms before his avowed schedule.

Tellegen closed in a road show in Chicago and was at liberty, waiting for the opening of a new production with Sarah Bernhardt. Nick and Lou were a handsome pair—gay, debonair, dashing. They hit it off well together. Nick admired the cultured tones of Tellegen's speaking voice and its projection.

He worried about his own use of English, which was unimportant around Blue Island, but not to him.

"Tell me the truth, Lou," he said to his new friend, "would you take me for a typical American?"

"No," Tellegen answered. "A new American."

"I don't understand."

"Well," Tellegen began, "your English is excellent and your grammar nearly perfect."

Nick demanded, "Then what is wrong?"

"The improper use of the present tense instead of the future is your only flaw."

Nick leaned forward attentively. "Give me an example."

The actor was lost in thought. Then he said, "You say, 'I meet you in Blue Island' instead of 'I will meet you in Blue Island.' And instead of 'will' you say 'weel.' But don't bother about it," Tellegen advised. "Women 'weel,' " he said, imitative of Nick, "think it cute."

Nick was pleased by Tellegen's frankness. "In the future I weel certainly correct this," he vowed.

He never did.

Three weeks after the opening of the opera season at the Auditorium—a marbled-hall structure boasting of intricate mosaic flooring and acoustical excellence—Tellegen told Nick that Mary Garden was appearing in *Salomé* and he had tickets. Would Nick do him the honor of being his guest? Nick was delighted to accept.

The pair enjoyed the performance to the hilt. They were captivated by the singing and dancing of Miss Garden, who had always insisted that patrons were to "come and see Mary Garden," not merely to "hear Mary Garden," and maintained she was a "singing actress."

Many failed to share the feelings of Nick and Tellegen. *Salomé* was ushered in with a storm of criticism from the moralists. Miss Garden became the center of a furor. Percy Hammond, the celebrated critic, called her "the feminine giantess

who doth bestride our operatic world," and of her performance wrote, ". . . a florid, excessive, unhampered tour de
force, lawless and inhuman."

Chicago Chief of Police LeRoy T. Stewart, who took time
off from catching criminals to catch a show now and then,
immediately established himself as a one-man censor. Crackled
the disturbed chief, "It was disgusting. Miss Garden wallowed
around like a cat in a bed of catnip. There was no art in her
dance that I could see. If the same show were produced on
Halsted Street the people would call it cheap, but over at the
Auditorium they say it is art. Black art, if art at all. I would
not call it immoral. I would say it was disgusting."

Arthur Burrage Farwell, President of the Chicago Law and
Order Group, was a man who devoted his physical energies to
bluenosing. Nothing, absolutely nothing, of a salacious nature
escaped his all-seeing eyes. He was the public protector of
morals. His opinion on *Salomé* was sought, and he was given a
complimentary ticket.

"I am a normal man," the city guardian of morals stated,
"but I would not trust myself to see a performance of *Salomé*."

Tellegen called him "Old Fartwell."

Naturally the production was a nightly sellout.

After the opera, over demitasses, Tellegen and Nick discussed the show, and the actor probed Nick for his comments
on the star.

Nick was full of praise. "A captivating creature of rare tal-
ents, whose acting tonight could cause red blood to drop from
the bronzed arteries of the Colossus of Rhodes, Helios the sun
god," he rattled off.

"Bravo!" Tellegen cried, applauding enthusiastically. The
actor in him inquired, "Care to do an encore?"

"No," Nick declined. "To me that about sums it up."

"By the way," Tellegen casually asked, "how brave are
you?"

"Exceedingly brave," Nick replied, "if the odds are in my favor."

"Would you be courageous enough to repeat your thumbnail description of Miss Garden to her face?"

Nick said, "I would welcome the chance to pay the lady a deserved compliment."

"You'll soon have that opportunity," Tellegen said enigmatically.

Three nights later the actor guided Nick to the dressing room of the famous Scottish soprano, and the young fig merchant, who rarely passed up a chance to drop a few pearls of self-conceived prose, reiterated the laudatory words.

"Wonderful," Miss Garden beamed. "You have the voice and manner of a poet."

Nick told her he was truly sorry for the opinions of a handful of critics and blamed the hue and cry on the ignorant.

"It is more than the ignorant," Miss Garden disagreed. "The ignorant I can understand by bowing down to reach their level. This criticism is from the illiterate. I thought the Dance of the Seven Veils was pure drama, but they . . . they"—anger crept into her voice—"compare it with the Folies Bergère."

She showed them a letter she had received from Oscar Hammerstein, whose Manhattan Opera Company had brought her to this country for roles in *Salomé, Louise, Thaïs* and *Pelléas et Mélisande.* Hammerstein had jocularly suggested that Miss Garden wear flannel petticoats in her veil dance, reminding her that she always had a deadly fear of getting cold feet.

They discussed opera, a subject on which Nick was well informed. During a pause in the conversation Miss Garden suddenly asked:

"Why isn't an attractive man like you married?"

Nick, slightly startled, quickly recovered. "There are many plateaus of intelligence," he said. "I know not on which one I stand. I do know that I can find no woman to stand on the same one with me."

Miss Garden snapped her fingers. "Your search is over."

"How so?"

Ignoring the question, Miss Garden inquired, "Does she have to be a Greek?"

"It matters not."

Miss Garden seemed pleased and said, "I have just the girl for you, then. She can not only stand on your plateau, as you put it, she might even stand on a slightly higher one and eventually pull you up to her level."

She jotted down the tricky spelling of "Dandolos," and his address. "You will hear from me," she concluded.

Miss Garden kept her word. Within a few days Nick received a brief and to-the-point note containing the name of a young lady, her address, and the date and the time he was expected to call at her residence. The note was written on perfumed stationery. He showed it to Lou Tellegen.

Tellegen sniffed the envelope, sighed ecstatically, and read the contents. He claimed he had heard of the young lady and knew something of her background.

Curiosity piqued, Nick asked his friend to brief him on the mystery girl. Tellegen refused to divulge his knowledge. All he would reveal was "She'll be a match for you—that I guarantee."

Nick dressed carefully for his first social engagement outside of the Blue Island sector. Which suit to wear was an easy decision: he had only two. After a careful whisk-broom brushing, he slipped into the blue-black one and chose an appropriate bow tie. He walked to a cab stand and gave the driver a Lake Shore Drive address.

The cabby microscopically examined his customer.

"You sure of that number, mister?"

Nick pulled Miss Garden's crumpled note from his pocket and strained to read it under the gaslight. "I'm sure."

The cab started up, the driver probably wondering why a man from the Blue Island neighborhood was going to the fashionable part of the city near Lake Michigan, where the millionaires lived.

Nick settled back in the seat. He hadn't ridden in many automobiles. Now they were becoming fairly commonplace, and he could barely walk a block without hearing the honking of a horn from one of the horseless carriages.

There was a time when these vehicles had been frowned upon. In 1902, acting on the complaints of horse-and-carriage owners and others who considered the motorized contraptions a menace to life and limb, the South Park Board banned them from Michigan Avenue, Jackson and Washington Parks, prohibiting all autos that "emit obnoxious odors" (gasoline cars) or "spurts of vapor" (steam cars), or cars "able to reach a speed exceeding eight miles per hour." In this same edict they banned all horns or whistles.

As the taxi puffed past a succession of millionaires' homes, Nick gazed out the window curiously and admiringly—yet not longingly—at the handsome edifices, little realizing that during the course of his life he was fated to make more money —an estimated $500 million—than these successful men earned in their productive periods of sweat and toil, and sometimes conniving.

The cab jarred to a stop before a lofty brownstone mansion that resembled a castle, with its balconies, turrets, minarets. A heavy iron picket fence surrounded the property.

The driver was still doubtful. "You sure this is the place?"

Nick noted the number on a costly mailbox, and said that it was. He alighted, paid his fare, overtipping the driver. The driver gasped a "Thanks" and drove away, now positive his passenger had made no mistake in the fashionable address.

He walked through the spacious grounds, treading on flagstone to the front door, and lifted a solid brass knocker, letting it fall back noisily into place. A butler opened the door and asked for his card. Nick saw no reason to hand him a business card that was probably stained from figs.

"Miss Parkinson is expecting me," he told the servant. Satisfied, the man ushered him into a gold and silver drawing room of French decor, and relieved him of his hat and coat. Nick sat down on a chaise longue, his descent made gradual by air in the couch cushions.

He looked about. The room had stained-glass windows, and Nick thought how beautiful the glass must appear when it came alive from the sun. The tapestries were rich and colorful. He knew they came from Europe. From where he sat he could see through an open doorway a circular staircase of carved wood winding up and away from his sight.

"Mr. Dandolos?"

A soft voice stirred him from his reveries. He rose to face the slim, blonde, creamy-complexioned girl who was destined to change the course of his life.

The Millionaire

NICK and Elizabeth Parkinson* had instant rapport. In their relationship the old world fused with the new to unite in an amalgam of European-American understanding. Both the young people had open minds thirsting for erudition, and as predicted by Mary Garden, they were ensconced on an intellectual plateau where each pulled the other across new thresholds of knowledge.

Nick contributed his profound lore of philosophy, discoursing on the early Greek scholars, running the gamut from Aristotle to Xenophon, exposing her to the science that investigates the facts and principles of reality, human nature, conduct, and logic. She absorbed his teachings and grasped the literal interpretation that philosophy could meet all the vicissitudes of life, enabling one to face them with calmness of temper and abstract judgment. And it dawned upon her that this was the key to Nick's behavior. For her part, she introduced him to English literature, to such poets and essayists as Byron, Keats, Shelley, Lamb, Coleridge, Cowper, Addison, Steele, Masefield, and Robert and Elizabeth Barrett Browning.

The retentive skills of Nick's memory and his fast assimila-

* A pseudonym. Mr. Dandolos preferred not to disclose her identity.

tion of tricky passages amazed the girl. She marveled at the
fact that after one reading of *Poetical Blossoms* (1633) by
Abraham Cowley, an English metaphysical poet, he was able
to recite it almost verbatim.

The pair were seldom out in public except for an occasional
stroll along the shores of Lake Michigan, the concert gardens,
or an opera.

One sunny May day Nick took Elizabeth on a tour of Blue
Island. The girl of enormous wealth and high breeding, whose
sheltered existence had blinded her to life on the so-called
other side of the tracks, was stunned by what she saw. It was
as if Nick had taken her to his native land.

One evening she said to him, "Nicholas, we really need few
divertissements. Just this chaise to sit on, a few books to read
to each other, and it really doesn't seem to matter what goes
on in the rest of the world."

Nick was falling in love. He realized the symptoms: the
pain, the ecstasy, the longing, the hours that passed as minutes.
To him Elizabeth was a princess, and he treated her like one.
And throughout the years he was to show respect and courtesy toward women, regardless of their stations in life. He believed that a queen holding a scepter and a scrubwoman holding a mop had much in common: both were women. He was
never to strike a woman, mistreat a woman, or use a woman to
further any schemes for personal gain. Even those who periodically took advantage of his generosity failed to disillusion
him or alter his feeling that women were essentially pleasure-
giving creatures, put upon the earth to comfort and refine
men. To him a man and a woman were dissimilar as night and
day. Mike Todd, the impresario, used to quote him: "If you
think you've had a logical argument with your wife—look
out! You've married a man by mistake."

Sleep was difficult with Elizabeth crowding his mind. He
mixed up several deliveries of figs and was guilty of some
bookkeeping errors.

His friend Chris sensed what was happening. "Go marry her," he suggested.

Shaking his head, Nick said sadly, "I think it would be impossible."

"Why?" Chris pressed.

Not one to gossip or divulge his business, Nick temporarily broke his rules by explaining, "The girl is rich. Not moderately rich. Very rich. And by comparison I am pretty poor, and . . ."

"A man in love," Chris interrupted.

"Desperately. Painfully."

"And suffering in the loins," Chris guessed.

Nick remained silent.

Chris slapped his thigh with an open palm. "I know just what you need," he said slyly.

Nick was attentive.

"The Everleigh Sisters."

"The Everleigh Sisters," Nick repeated, awe in his voice.

"That's what I said."

"I haven't that kind of money," Nick stated.

Chris said that he did, due to a very lucky night at Barbudi. He had won over $100 and wanted Nick to be his guest; they would both sin in a deluxe manner. He tried some logic. "It will in no way affect your position of love with Miss Parkinson. Quite the contrary, it might strengthen it. You need the Everleigh Sisters for medicinal reasons. You are undergoing sexual privations that touch the nerve ends and make you jumpy. The Everleigh Sisters will restore your health and calm you."

Nick consented. "Anything you prescribe, Doctor," he said amiably.

The Everleigh Club, two sumptuous connected mansions operated by the sisters Ada and Minna Everleigh, was located in the levee district, a name derived from Southern gamblers who, sensing a bonanza in wide-open Chicago, had migrated to the city. Pleasure seekers could find nearly two hundred brothels in this entertainment belt, ranging in price from one to fifty dollars.

The Everleigh Club had a fifty dollar minimum.

In those days houses of assignation were plentiful and famous in America, and their names dropped from the tongues of travelers established the speakers as men of the world. There were Josie Arlington and Belle Anderson in New Orleans; Frisco Tessie in San Francisco; Babe Conners, the dusky St. Louis madame; Mahogany Hall located in Washington, D.C.; Rose Bailey, New York; Rose Hicks, Philadelphia; Annie Chambers, Kansas City; Minnie Stevens, Boston; Belle Stewart, Pittsburgh; dark-skinned Carrie Watson, Chicago.

All had something in common: lack of class.

Then the Everleigh Sisters arrived in Chicago, equipped with Southern drawls and grandiose schemes to open their establishment at 2131–33 South Dearborn Street. Minna was twenty-one, Ada twenty-three. They were gorgeously gowned in the latest Parisian originals, created especially for them. The girls were busy, beautiful, business-wise. They changed men's entire conception of a house of prostitution.

The Everleigh Sisters catered to gentlemen only: no rowdies or ruffians, no drunks, no shirtsleeves, no beer drinkers. They wanted—and got—the champagne sippers at a tariff of $12 per bottle. On a busy night the popping of corks made some think the Civil War was being refought. The clientele consisted of roués, ne'er-do-wells, landed gentry, just plain millionaires, occasional royalty, and a few nonentities such as Nick and Chris who managed to crash the club portals.

The Everleigh Club opened its doors on January 1, 1900, and ran until 1911, at which time the doors were bolted and the windows shuttered by reformers. The sisters were rumored to have retired with a million dollars in cash, plus a fortune in jewelry, art, and tapestries.

The consensus was that they deserved every cent of it. No

patron of the Everleigh Club was ever shortchanged in value received.

Although they did not know it, Nick and the Everleigh Sisters were to have much in common. Nick virtually lifted the game of craps from its knees in back alleys to an atmosphere of luxury in plush gambling resorts. The Everleigh Sisters elevated the world's oldest profession from sordid surroundings to palaces. To pay them a visit was a costly pleasure.

The young ladies in the Everleigh manse were under the expert tutelage of the sisters. It was firmly impressed upon them that they were ladies and must act like ladies at all times, regardless of difficult situations. Lectures were delivered on conduct, hygiene, patience, and politeness. To encourage the girls to read, a well-stocked library, including books on etiquette, was installed.

Meanwhile, Minna, the practical sister, would constantly remind her charges, "Remember—the Everleigh Club cannot waste time on a man without a checkbook."

The numerous parlors competed with one another for prizes in grandeur. The Copper Room, the Silver Room, the Oriental Room, the Egyptian Room, the Chinese Room, the Moorish Room, the Gold Room, the Red Room, the Green Room, and the Rose Room were some of the titles of these spacious chambers. A tipsy patron, lost in the maze of rooms, was overheard to remark to a friend in the same condition, "They got all these expensive rooms, but where in the hell is the bathroom?"

Carpeting was extra thick. Potted palms were omnipresent. So were statues of Greek goddesses. The two buildings housing the Club were joined together in such a way that twin mahogany staircases were at opposite ends of the lower floor. Downstairs there was gourmet dining resembling a Roman feast, a half hour of gambling nightly (with no house cut), music and entertainment. A $15,000 gold piano was the talk of the town. To incur the wrath of the sisters one had only to set a drink on its costly top.

Also the talk of the town, mostly emanating from wives, were the bedrooms upstairs.

Special rooms were the Gold, Silver, and Copper ones, reserved for millionaires and visiting royalty only. Money was a crass word never mentioned until the guest was ready for departure. Some paid as dearly as $1,000 for an evening of food, entertainment, and fleshly titillations. None complained of the charges.

It was on the fringe of this atmosphere that Nick and Chris found themselves. After ringing the doorbell, they were admitted by a liveried Negro servant who kept them in a waiting room, hesitant about taking their hats and coats until inspection by one of the sisters.

Minna, the red-haired one with the gray-blue eyes, came forward. "I trust you gentlemen have the proper introductions," she inquired in purring tones.

Chris, who was under the false impression that it was what he had in his wallet that counted, blurted, "We have plenty of money."

"Money is not of primary importance here," Miss Everleigh hastily replied. "We put more stock in breeding." She waited.

The door had been left partially open and Nick, his eyes wandering past it, remarked, "Isn't that a statue of Daphne?"

"Why, yes," Miss Everleigh said, somewhat surprised, and asked, "Are you an expert on sculpture, Mister . . . Mister . . . ?"

"Dandolos." Nick supplied the name and bowed before her. Straightening up, he answered, "Not exactly an expert, madame, except that I know if that is Daphne then Apollo must be near."

Minna smiled. "You are familiar with the legend, then?"

"Certainly," Nick said. "Daphne attracted the love of

Apollo, who pursued her. To escape she offered prayers and was changed into a laurel tree."

Miss Everleigh was delighted. "Sir, you have a profound knowledge of mythology."

"And with your kind permission, madame," Nick said, indicating the doorway leading into the club's interior, "I would like to leave the world of mythology for one of reality."

"Follow me, gentlemen," Miss Everleigh said.

Chris gave Nick a congratulatory pat on the back. They passed a statute of Apollo. Three orchestras were playing in separate rooms. Nick wandered around. He came to a room where several tables had been pushed together and cloths draped over them. Large denominations of paper money dotted the surface, and dice were being thrown. Nick watched, absorbed, his eyes on the excitement-flushed faces of the players.

A short time later Ada Everleigh appeared and issued an order: "One last roll, gentlemen."

There were mild protests and a few groans. The next shooter rolled an eight, quickly followed by a seven, and the gambling ended. Nick couldn't understand the reasoning behind the abbreviated actions. This was a house of pleasure, and judging by the faces of the players, they were enjoying themselves. Why stop them then? He sought out Ada to ask her about the sudden termination of the game.

She answered in a speech that sounded as if she had given it many times before:

"Gambling, we have discovered, is the strongest influence in the life of any man. No woman can compete with cards or dice, particularly if they be for high stakes. Men will push women from their laps at the first sound of dice or the shuffle of cards; and I would not be surprised," she whispered, partially concealing her face behind a hand-painted fan, "if they would rush from warm, perfumed beds to shake those ivories." She lowered the fan. "That is why I allow only half an hour of gambling. Then the men's desires for women are re-kindled."

Nick received much food for thought that night at the Everleigh Club. Later, upstairs, he also received the young, firm body of a girl named Judy. The girl simulated warmth and passion, but Nick performed in a perfunctory manner.

The Everleigh Sisters had coached their ladies of the evening to act conscientiously in the giving of pleasures. Judy had tried with Nick, but was well aware she had failed to rouse her client to any degree. However, she felt she could justify her ineffectualness.

She approached Minna, who was often confidante to the problems of her stable. "I had a queer bird last night," she said.

"In what way?" Minna asked.

"Well, I had this tall, dark fellow. He was real handsome. You know how you teach us to talk with men so they won't think everything is business?"

Minna nodded and waited for her to continue.

"I asked this man if he was ever in love. He said that he had been in love with the same person since he was twelve years old. I said she must have been very pretty for a love to last all those years. I'll never forget his answer. Positively never.

"He said, 'It wasn't a she, but a bearded he—and his name was Homer.'"

Minna burst into gales of unrestrained laughter. It must have been that intelligent Mr. Dandolos, she surmised.

"Whatever is so funny, Miss Minna?" Judy demanded.

She explained, "Homer was a learned Greek."

"What business was he in?"

"Poetry."

"Sounds like monkey business, if you ask me," Judy said with a toss of her head. "It's hard enough for us to make an honest living without competition from men."

* * *

With each succeeding visit Elizabeth and Nick were drawn closer together. Both were undergoing intense physical strain. The fires of pure passion were a consuming flame to the girl, but in those days maidens from the better families were severely chaste. The loss of virginity was an unthinkable wanton act, wherein the male participant was generally regarded as a "horrible beast." Wedlock was the only legitimate and honorable road leading to a bed.

Marriage was discussed. Two formidable obstacles loomed in the pathway: a simpering mother, behind whose façade of a false smile was an agile mind that sloped on the interests of her daughter; and a male parent—a titan of the meat-packing business, firm, unyielding, decision-making, a controller of the lives of hundreds of servile employees.

Nick told Elizabeth, "To win over your parents and gain their consent will be more monumental a task than ever confronted the Greeks battling the Turks."

It was fairly early in the evening, and Elizabeth's parents were home. The time, the girl believed, was propitious for Nick to strike. She dropped her hand to his wrist, fingers closing around it, long, tapering nails digging into his skin—a sword prick to jar her knight into combat.

"Talk with them now, Nicholas."

Nick had been smoking an expensive cigar. It had cost him ten cents and was Cuban-made. Stubbing it out in the ashtray, he said, "Bring them in, Elizabeth."

Within a few minutes Elizabeth returned with her parents and, excusing herself, left the room. Mr. and Mrs. Franklin Parkinson seated themselves facing Nick. Up to the present their conversations with him had been strictly desultory.

"Mr. and Mrs. Parkinson," Nick addressed them in a clear voice, "I would be most honored and gratified if you would grant me permission to marry your daughter Elizabeth."

A slight gasp came from Mrs. Parkinson, the color slowly draining from her cheeks. Her husband clamped his jaws tightly. His eyes narrowed to pinpoints. Turning to his wife, he said, "I'll take care of this matter, my dear."

Without a word Mrs. Parkinson rose, straightened out her wide skirt, and left the room, closing the door behind her. Neither Nick nor Mr. Parkinson immediately spoke. The air seemed electrically charged. Mr. Parkinson began pacing slowly, deliberately, soundlessly in front of Nick, who sat motionless. It was the same tactic he used with his board of directors before attempting to win their approval. Finally he halted and faced the youth who had asked for the hand in marriage of his only daughter.

"What is your income, my boy?" he asked abruptly.

Nick revealed its lowly extent.

"And your future prospects?"

Nick admitted they were not too rosy where the making of any vast sum of money was concerned.

Thanking him for the honesty of his self-appraisal, Mr. Parkinson inquired, "What is your object in life, Mr. Dandolos?"

"To seek the truth, sir."

Mr. Parkinson bristled. Then he took a deep breath and counted to five, a system he had developed for maintaining self-control. Maddening thoughts were spinning through his head, such as, Here is a crazy Greek, barely a citizen, whose object in life is to seek the truth instead of seeking a fortune. Just another mad foreigner. This boy should be out where opportunity beckons, shirtsleeves rolled up, working by the sweat of his brow as I once did!

"Is this seeking the truth you speak of an original thought?" Mr. Parkinson asked.

"No, sir," Nick said, "it belonged to Plato."

An idea popped into Mr. Parkinson's head. Why not offer the boy a job, then give him some backbreaking menial work that would force him into quitting?

"Would you like to work for me, Mr. Dandolos?" Mr. Parkinson asked, certain the answer would be yes.

"Thank you, but no, sir," Nick declined.

Mr. Parkinson was amazed. "For any particular reason?"

"I am an animal lover, Mr. Parkinson, although I am certainly anything but a vegeterian. Full well do I realize that it is necessary to slaughter these animals you own for human consumption, but I wouldn't care to be connected, even remotely, with any business that ultimately destroyed them."

Mr. Parkinson was momentarily stunned. To him, a steak was a steak—something highly desirable to grace anyone's plate. Who would ever consider the dumb cow that was butchered? Well, evidently this odd boy from Greece did.

"You wouldn't care to be in any business that destroyed a cow?" Mr. Parkinson said, barely able to control his anger.

"That's the way I feel, sir."

"And how do you feel about my daughter?"

"I love her."

"How deeply?"

"I would give my life for her."

"Humph," Mr. Parkinson snorted. "Sounds very romantic . . . very brave. But no substance. I don't think you're very practical, Mr. Dandolos."

"You are correct in your assumptions, sir," Nick agreed. He relit his cigar.

"But still you want to marry my daughter and take her away from all this?" He waved his arm about to indicate the vastness of his possessions.

Nick smiled faintly. "If she will accept my way of life."

"*Your* way of life," Mr. Parkinson mocked in a tone of ridicule. "And what is that?" He did not wait for an answer, but went on, "A few figs sold here and there? Raising my grandson in some squalid surroundings? No, sir. Not for my Elizabeth. She deserves far better."

Nick asked calmly, "Specifically, just what do you want for your daughter, Mr. Parkinson?"

"Money," Mr. Parkinson snapped. "An accumlation of it known as wealth. I want her to have every luxury possible—which is something she has now."

"Then I will secure it for her."

Mr. Parkinson laughed derisively. "Just like that," he said, snapping his fingers. "You make it sound simple. How will you raise it?"

"I'll have to give the matter some thought."

"Considerable thought, I would say," Mr. Parkinson said mockingly.

Nick was never too pleased discussing any financial matters. But now it was vital to his future happiness. He asked, "How much money would be required to make you . . . er . . . I mean your daughter, happy?" The word slip had been a deliberate one.

This was Mr. Parkinson's chance to sweep the Greek youth from his daughter's life and open the door for wealthy suitors. Chuckling to himself, he named what he considered an impossible figure: "One million dollars."

He stared at Nick, certain he would find shock symptoms. The youth, however, displayed no emotion; he was as self-contained as if some negligible sum had been mentioned. He lit another cigar with steady fingers, and asked, "How long a time will you extend me to raise this amount?"

What an utter fool this boy is, Mr. Parkinson thought. True, America was a land of opportunity, but this fig-selling immigrant would have a difficult time surviving and being able to afford a decent marble tombstone when he died, let alone making a million dollars.

"One year from today," Mr. Parkinson said lightly.

Nick whipped out a small notebook, recorded the current date and year. Slipping it into his pocket, he said, "I'll take the gamble, sir."

Mr. Parkinson generalized, "All you Greeks are gamblers, aren't you?"

"No, sir," Nick returned. "There were Valerius, Lycurgus, Laberius, Italicus, Cato . . ."

"Please—that's enough," Mr. Parkinson said, halting the flow of names. He constructed an equation: "One year, plus one million dollars, equals Elizabeth." He was delighted with his shrewdness and the hard bargain he had driven. He had rid himself of this Greek fortune hunter once and for all. He nodded curtly to Nick and left.

Elizabeth returned. Her father had been smiling as she passed him in the hallway. Nick's face, she noted, was also wreathed in smiles. It all seemed to add up to a satisfactory arrangement. Rushing up to Nick, she threw her arms around him, burying her head against his shoulder, and asked hopefully, "Is everything favorable, darling?"

He stroked her hair and fondled an earlobe. "Everything is fine," he told her.

"You reached an understanding with Daddy?"

"More or less of an agreement."

"Do you want to tell me about it, Nicholas?"

"No," Nick said.

"But—but, I——"

He kissed her to smother the words. "Just have patience," he said.

She had dozens of questions to ask. Chief among them was "When can we marry?"

"Within a year at the latest," Nick assured her. Drawing her to him, he kissed her long and tenderly. "That was for goodnight," he said. "I must go home now."

"But it's early, dear," Elizabeth protested.

Nick said, "I'm going to be up all night."

"Doing what?"

"Thinking." He put on his hat and coat, and she walked him to the front door, where he paused to remark, "One of your famous Americans, Benjamin Franklin, once wrote, 'Plough deep while sluggards sleep.' "

"Happy ploughing," she said, waving as he walked away from the mansion. She made no attempt to fathom the quotation from Benjamin Franklin, knowing that Nick must have had a valid reason for recalling it.

The next morning Mr. Matsoukas, a lower-floor tenant, approached Nick's landlady. His face was haggard. "Doesn't the man over me ever sleep?" he asked, adding, "All night he walked. Back and forth . . . back and forth. He must have worn a path in your carpet."

"Oh, my," wailed the landlady, "it was practically new when I rented him the room."

It was true Nick had walked the floor until five A.M., his mind congested by thoughts of how to make a million dollars in twelve months. By dawn he arrived at a definite conclusion: he had no chance of achieving success in a commerical enterprise without the necessary capital, and even if he had backing, it would be suffocatingly boring. There must be a way— some way—to make fast legitimate money involving thrills, excitement, and speculation.

A few ideas were rattling around in the back of his head, and one in particular he believed was worthy to discuss with King George. King George was a late riser. It was two in the afternoon when Nick finally gained an audience with him. They talked for three solid, uninterrupted hours. The subject, introduced by Nick, was horse racing.

He had attended the races only once—Derby Day at Washington Park, just before the track temporarily closed. The featured race was called the American Derby. Here, among the crowd, he saw the cream of Chicago society clad in all their finery. For him to stretch his arms in any direction and not touch a millionaire was difficult.

Nick devoured the fashionable spectacle, showing scant interest in the racing card itself. He did, however, hand a bookmaker two dollars, betting on a horse to win. The odds were 8–1. He had no particular reason for betting this horse.

It finished last.

King George talked to Nick in a fatherly fashion, trying to discourage what he called "the wildest and most presumptuous idea I ever heard," of making a million dollars in one year, by a neophyte who didn't know a filly from a mare, a wither from a fetlock, or the sound of a neigh from a whinny. He spoke of the many pitfalls of racing, the disillusionments, the recriminations and remorse, the sufferings in general.

Nick listened carefully, undiscouraged. "Humanity," he told King George, "has but one objective: to suffer. This will never happen to me."

During the last few minutes of the polemics, King George, who considered the chances of horse players winning large sums almost infinitesimal, conceded, "Of course, it *is* possible, Nick, but the odds against reaching your goal are enormous."

Nick replied, "Odds are set by humans in order to be beaten by humans."

When he found it was impossible to dissuade him, King George advised Nick to have his fling, but at the Canadian tracks: Montreal, Toronto, Ottawa. Here, King George figured, a man would be privileged to more inside information, especially on a "boat" (fixed) race. Also, there was a better chance that bookmakers, being far from infallible, might make mistakes in figuring the odds and a smart bettor could pounce upon their errors for a killing.

Nick went into a period of deep study. It was as if he were an undergraduate again, taking only a single course, not to be found in any college curriculum, that might be titled How to Beat the Races. So occupied was he that he was able to visit Elizabeth only periodically. Piled in his furnished room were hundreds of copies, both current and past, of the Daily Racing Form, established in 1896 and a bible for horse bettors. He also made up his own charts, which were clear and concise.

Although only a neophyte in experience, he already enjoyed certain advantages over expert horse pickers and veteran newspaper handicappers: his photographic memory and the natural gift he possessed of total recall. The speed of his assimilation was phenomenal. In no time at all he learned of horses' sex, age, color, racing habits, etc. He even recognized the names of pidgelings (half-castrated animals).

It took him less than a two-day investigation of the perils and risks of betting systems to discard them. At first glance, systems beckoned and invited and almost guaranteed earnings. It was comparable to accepting a gold-carded invitation to success. True, he admitted, some might even work, and a disciplined bettor, by sticking to one ritualistically, could conceivably show a daily profit. That was when the danger signs began flickering. If the system started to enrich the player, his confidence and ego could rise to a point where he no longer considered it necessary, discarding it like a crutch. But the worst thing about a system, Nick discovered, was that it converted the player into an automaton, and when this happened a gambler became regimented and lost his individuality. The only point Nick admired in a system was that it ruled out "intuitive" and "hunch" bettors.

Part of Nick's classwork came from probing the inveterate horse players to separate the compulsive and chronic from the shrewd and calculating gamblers. Many foolish followers of the horses, at the end of a winning day, made such statements to him as "I had on my lucky cuff links" or "My good old rabbit's foot came through for me." Talismans, amulets, charms, or fetishes could, he was positive, possess no extraordinary powers to avert losses, but could provide a measure of confidence leading to higher betting. To Nick these were pure, unadulterated poppycock. Superstitions, he believed, were for the savages in darkest Africa.

Nick was, when fame descended upon him, considered the only big plunger in history who had not a single superstition.

Someone once said, "The only way to beat the races is to play the winners," and that was precisely what Nick intended to do. It was the overlooked horse that he searched for . . . somewhere between the "can't lose" ones and the "long-shots," and ranging from 3–1 to 5–1 in price.

He started paying daily visits to the track, but showing strong restraint, made only "mind" bets. He always went alone. When Chris, a confirmed girl chaser, asked him about the fair sex at the track, Nick replied, "You'll never find a beautiful horse player—too much studying of the Racing Form causes wrinkles."

Years later at Aqueduct, he stated, "A woman could walk naked here ten minutes before post time and she'd be safer than riding in a Brinks truck with two eunuchs."

After three months of intensive study, Nick felt that he was ready for his final exams, the racetrack to be testing ground. He planned to do something considered foolish by any turf follower: bet on every race, the same amount of money, across the board. Should he come close to breaking even he would feel he had graduated with honors.

At the end of the racing day he returned to Blue Island with a profit of $208. He graduated *cum laude*.

The next day he told Elizabeth good-bye, packed a single suitcase, sold his fig business to a competitor, stuffed a copy of Plato's *Dialogues* into a coat pocket, and boarded a train for Montreal, Canada.

As the eastbound train skirted the southern end of Lake Michigan to chug into Indiana, Nick relaxed in the observation car, puffing on a fat cigar, his mind reverting to Archimedes, Greek mathematician, physicist, and inventor, who once stated, "Give me a place to stand, and I will move the earth."

Nick's ambitions were not quite so lofty as were those of the Greek who had lived and died before the birth of Christ. He had no plans for moving the earth. His were more modest: to destroy a few bookmakers.

He checked into a single room at the Mont Royal Hotel. The next day found him at the track. These were the days of the handbooks that would eventually become targets for storms of criticism and be driven out of business to be replaced by a frigid, meticulous, never-erring device: the totalizer. As Nick fondly recalled, "There was more warmth in the clasp of a bookmaker's clammy hand than in all the electrically controlled numerals flashing on the board."

In the olden—and as some might phrase them, "golden"— years of racing, it was possible for everyone at the track to go home a winner and the bookmakers to go home bankrupt. This happened four times during a single week at an Eastern track. Some bookmakers were seen weeping openly and unashamedly. They received little sympathy.

"Finding a single tear on a bookmaker's cheek is comparable to finding the Holy Grail," Nick always contended. Those halcyon days for the customers are buried in the archives of horse racing lore. Too often now the state emerges as the only solid winner at day's end. Pari-mutuel betting isn't really gambling, by any stretch of the imagination; the handicap of percentages eliminates that. Besides, there's no margin for error. The fun has been deleted. Continued perfection from the tote board can become a crashing bore.

In those dear departed days the bookmakers congregated in a section known as "the ring," each with a little stall and a chalk board to mark the odds he was willing to give the public. These were obtained from his own head or from a professional pricemaker who designed them to give the bookmakers an edge.

Should he not care for the prices offered, the discerning bettor could shop around, wandering from stall to stall, until he found the figures satisfactory. It was competitive in the "good old American way." Prices, depending on how the money flowed, would rise and fall. Mistakes were infrequent but costly. Sometimes two horses having similar sounding names were confused and the wrong prices chalked up. After such errors were committed, the astute bettor like Nick would step in to lay down an enormous wager.

At the start Nick bet conservatively, feeling his way along, and at the same time picking up pointers and gaining knowledge through practical experience. His bankroll—a large slice of which he kept in his pocket—steadily grew. Thus far he had not taken any big plunge to lay down a huge amount of money on a single race.

What he needed, he felt, was inside information.

One of the leading jockeys of the period was Phil Musgrave, a thoroughly honest rider, but one who could often pass along tips that were invaluable to Nick. Nothing escaped Musgrave. He seemed to have an ear against every stable door. He would talk with Nick by the hour, pouring forth his knowledge of the sport of kings and acquainting him with some of the common sharp practices that he ofttimes detected.

Among these were:

Holding a horse back at the post.

Weighting down the shoes of a horse.

Sneaking into a stall and sitting on a horse all night; by morning the animal would be tired.

Stealing a horse from his stall during the night and running him on paved roads for five or six miles in a strenuous workout.

Slipping a horse some extra food just prior to a race, which would create a sluggishness and consequently slow down the animal.

Changing shoes to put different-weight ones on each hoof, causing the horse to wobble when running.

Driving a nail into a horse's foot.

Placing a small battery beneath the saddle under the pommel pad, thus being able to give the horse an electric jolt to increase his speed.

Narcotics—a "needle" to hypo the horse into extra speed, and a narcotic in powder form to slow him down.

Ganging up on a favorite. Holding him back in the stretch by locking the leg of the rival jockey with his own.

Nick now began betting heavily. Within five months his bankroll swelled to nearly $400,000. His heavy speculations attracted the attention of the Daily Racing Form, and this publication, writing on his ventures, dubbed him "Nick the Greek." The nickname stuck with him until his death.

Overnight he became a celebrity. A "Nick the Greek Tip Sheet" was hawked at all the leading tracks. Dozens of players followed him around the ring, trying to eavesdrop on his betting. Touts stuck to him like glue, hoping he'd drop the name of a horse that they could pass on to prospective customers by saying, "Nick the Greek told me it looks like a winner."

Nick had nothing against touts. As a matter of fact, he had inadvertently created one. He was dining alone in the Mont Royal Hotel. When the check arrived he paid the bill in cash. Of course, he could have signed a chit, but he had strong aversions to putting his name to anything. "The easiest way to stay out of trouble is to have arthritic fingers," he used to say.

The waiter brought him a sheaf of bills in change, and as Nick was riffling through the currency to find a suitable tip, the waiter made a request.

"Never mind tipping me, Mr. Dandolos—just give me one of your selections for tomorrow."

Nick was fond of this particular waiter, a jolly fellow who always radiated happiness and, what was more important, never forgot to fill a half-empty water glass. He hovered over the American like a mother hen, advising against certain dishes, suggesting others.

"Bring me a pencil and paper and I'll see what I can do for you," Nick instructed.

Nick closed his eyes, bent his head slightly, and jogged his memory to recall the entries on tomorrow's card. Handed a pencil and paper, he jotted down the name of a horse in each of the eight races. The waiter thanked him profusely.

The following evening when Nick returned from the track, there was a case of French champagne in his room and a card reading: "With deepest appreciation and thanks for what you did for me. Jacques duWayne."

Nick could not recall having ever done favors for a man bearing the name of duWayne. It was an unusual name and he would have remembered. Puzzled, and certain a mistake had been made, he was about to telephone the desk when there was a knock on his door. He opened it to confront an impeccably dressed man.

"I guess you don't recognize me," the caller said.

Nick searched his face. "No," he said.

"I'm your former waiter, Jacques duWayne."

Inviting him in, Nick inquired of his sudden prosperity. The man explained, *"You're* my benefactor, Mr. Dandolos. Every horse you gave me was a winner. Eight in a row. I bet each one on the nose and had them hooked up in many parlays. You want to know how much I made, thanks to you?"

Nick didn't particularly care, but knew there was no way he could stop this enthusiastic Frenchman from telling him. So to be courteous, he feigned interest.

"Ten thousand dollars!"

Nick congratulated him on his good fortune and opened a bottle of warm champagne. He took only a few sips. Jacques duWayne finished the bottle, spoke of how he had quit his job, thanked Nick effusively again, and bid him good night.

Ten years later Nick was at Belmont. A tout edged up to him and whispered hoarsely out of the corner of his mouth, "I got one that can't lose in the fifth."

Very few track touts ever tried touting Nick because they invariably recognized him. Whenever he appeared at a track or a gambling casino, word spread with the speed of a prairie fire that "Nick the Greek is here!" But this tout hadn't bothered to look at his face, and when he finally did, his mouth dropped open in amazement as he exclaimed, "Mr. Dandolos!"

It was Jacques duWayne. His clothes were seedy, his eyes furtive—a combination indigenous to many touts who are afraid track police are breathing down their necks.

Nick slipped him a hundred dollar bill.

At the Montreal track Nick was finding it increasingly difficult to make bets without an immediate lowering of the odds. One day a favorite, who looked like he could run backwards and still win, opened at even money and appeared headed for an even lower drop in price. Nick decided to test his powers. He merely mentioned to several touts that there was another horse in the race whose speed he believed had been overlooked by the bookmakers.

The information tip whirled around the grandstand, borne from mouth to mouth. The animal had opened at 18–1. Suddenly it went to 10–1. Rumors reached Nick that the horse had been given "foo-foo dust," a powdered narcotic. The price dropped to 2–1 and the favorite went to 3–1, at which price Nick bet $10,000 on its nose. The favorite won by only a head over the horse Nick had touted, which was closing fast, causing Nick to lose none of his betting followers.

To obtain better odds, Nick organized a betting network in New Orleans, New York, Detroit, Chicago, Ottawa, and Toronto. So far away were these bets that comeback money failed to affect the odds.

He also decided to enter the bookmaking business, utilizing the services of two honest friends, Jim Devlin and a man known merely as Max the German. They opened shop at different stalls in the ring at Montreal. None knew they were controlled by Nick. By placing bets himself with competitive books, he would purposely influence prices on his own.

He then completed the full cycle by purchasing a horse and changing its name to Philosopher. A steeplechaser, the animal was registered under his friend Chris's name in Chicago. Philosopher was clocked in fast time in workouts, but when he went to the post the first time for Nick he finished dead last.

Losing money on the race didn't bother Nick, but the poor showing of Philosopher did. He ordered the trainer to examine the horse carefully and call in a vet to find a reason for the poor performance. The vet discovered a loose nail in a shoe that had been pricking Philosopher.

Needing only a killing to reach his goal of a million dollars, Nick meant to attain it with Philosopher the next time out. To get better odds, the regular jockey was removed for the race and an apprentice substituted.

Philosopher opened at 100–1. Nick bet $50,000, spread around his U.S. and Canadian contacts for show. If the horse finished in the money, Nick intended closing out his racing operations and heading for Chicago, where he would show Mr. Parkinson one million dollars and marry his daughter. In other words, this could be it—the moment of truth!

Nick, a cigar held lightly in his mouth, seemed the portrait of a man without a care in the world as he sat in a box with the president of the Canadian Racing Association and other officials of the turf organization, calmly awaiting the running of the steeplechase. Close friends of his, they knew nothing of his bookmaking activities, price manipulations in other cities, or ownership of Philosopher. They only knew him to be a heavy bettor.

As the horses left the post and the Frenchmen in the crowd cried, "*Ils sont partis!*" Nick was busy flicking some spilled ashes from his sleeve. He didn't even focus his eyes on the race until the horses were at the quarter pole.

"Difficult to pick any horse in a steeplechase," he heard someone remark. "Much too risky."

Nick didn't think so.

Philosopher was bunched in the center of the pack at the three-quarter pole. One horse had fallen and another thrown its rider. In the stretch Philosopher came on fast, moving into third place, a position he clung to across the finish line. Nick stood up, stretched, and reached into his pocket for a handkerchief. As he pulled it out a Canadian twenty-five cent piece, caught in the folds of the linen, fell, striking against the wooden flooring with a ringing sound.

Nick got down on his hands and knees, searched for a full minute before giving up. A friend, noticing the disappearance of the coin, said comfortingly, "Hard luck, Nick."

"Yes," Nick observed sadly. "Lady Luck is a fickle goddess who doesn't seem inclined to favor me today."

He headed for the stables where he borrowed a laundry bag from a trainer. Then he walked to the bookmaking ring and collected $135,000 from five disgruntled bookies, stuffing the oversized Canadian paper money into the laundry bag and slinging it over his shoulder.

At the entrance to the track he hailed a cab. As he climbed in he heard someone laughing in a raucous voice, "There goes Nick the Greek with his laundry."

In the hotel room he tossed the currency-filled bag on a bed. Jim Devlin and Max the German came in with the day's bookmaking profits. Their money was folded into neat stacks of the same denominations, held together by thick rubber bands. Nick untied the strings of the laundry bag, dumping the contents onto the bed. The bills were badly crumpled.

"I can't take them to the bank in this condition," Nick said. His plan was to exchange them for larger-denomination bills.

Max suggested, "We can hand fold the creases out."

Nick shook his head. "Take too long."

Devlin came up with an idea. "Let's get an ironing board and an iron, and press them."

"Fine," Nick said. Telephoning the linen room, he spoke to the housekeeper and ordered an iron and ironing board sent to Room 416.

There was a moment of silence on the other end of the wire.

At length the housekeeper said, "Sorry, sir, no cooking or ironing in the rooms. Strictly against hotel rules."

"Madame," Nick said softly, "do you think the rule could be broken just this once for, say, fifty dollars?"

"The iron and board will be up in five minutes," came the rapid reply.

At five in the morning Nick, Jim, and Max finished pressing the last bill and placing it in the correct pile on the bed. Jim and Max, exhausted from the night's work, lit cigarettes and sprawled in chairs. Nick appeared fresh. For half an hour he had been doing some calculating. When the money came in from the other tracks and he paid off the men working for him, his bankroll would stand at about one million, two hundred dollars.

He announced his retirement plans to Jim and Max, refuted their arguments with better ones of his own, and then made a request of Devlin.

"Jim, could you lend me a thousand dollars?"

"Sure," Jim said, counting out the money and handing it to Nick, never questioning the odd favor. The truth was that Nick needed some cash for his hotel bill and traveling expenses. Oh, he was worth a million dollars—no doubt of it— but after packing that amount neatly in a suitcase for Mr. Parkinson to count, it would leave him rather strapped.

A bellboy knocked on the door, handed Nick a telegram. It was signed by his close friend, the president of the Canadian Racing Association. The contents made it crystal clear that the Association had in some manner learned of Nick's bookmaking, betting operations, and horse ownership:

THE CANADIAN THOROUGHBRED HORSE RACING ASSOCIATION HAS UNANIMOUSLY VOTED TO BAN YOU FROM ALL CANADIAN TRACKS, EFFECTIVE TODAY, APRIL 12, 1912.

"Perfect timing," Nick commented, showing the telegram to Jim and Max.

One week later he was to receive another telegram, and again, like its predecessor, the timing was perfect. His winning money had come in from other cities. He was whistling cheerfully while he packed two suitcases. One was the same piece of luggage he had brought from Chicago that contained his meager belongings, mostly necessities. These had not expanded. The other suitcase contained the million dollars.

Someone was knocking. Nick dropped a shirt into the suitcase and, still whistling, flung the door open. A bellboy handed him a telegram. Nick gave the boy five dollars and closed the door against the effusive thanks.

He ripped open the envelope, read the contents, and the schemes and hopes of Nicholas Andrea Dandolos were shattered by the message on the yellow paper. He read it again and again until his eyes blurred, and tears—the first since boyhood—cascaded down his cheeks. The fingers holding the wire opened, and it fluttered to the floor, face up. Nick looked down at the typewritten words.

REGRET TO INFORM YOU THAT OUR BELOVED ELIZABETH PASSED AWAY LAST NIGHT.

FRANKLIN PARKINSON.

Nick stooped to pick up the telegram. Holding it at arms' length as if it were a poisonous serpent, he carried the piece of paper across the room to the open window. Balling the fingers of his right hand into a fist, he punched a hole in the screen. Reaching through it, he dropped the telegram, a gust of wind swirling it around the corner of the building.

He remained standing at the window, disturbed thoughts bouncing crazily through his grief-stricken mind. Then slowly and deliberately he removed the screen and laid it on the floor. Traffic noises drifted up from the street, four floors below. Another sound would be heard down there soon, an alien one that wasn't going to blend with the others—the sound of a body smashing into the pavement.

He started to raise a foot toward the window sill when a few lines from the *Dialogues* of Plato flashed into his memory.

Man is a prisoner who has no right to open the door of his prison and run away. . . . A man should wait, and not take his own life until God summons him.

Reaching up, he seized the window top and banged it down hard, cracking the glass. Going to the suitcase containing the million dollars, he stuffed as many of the bills into his pockets as they would hold.

Then he went downstairs and into the hotel bar.

Dropping into a seat at a small table, he said to the waiter, "Brandy. Metaxas brandy. Bring the bottle, please."

The waiter placed the bottle of brandy alongside Nick and poured an ounce of it into his glass. Nick, always a sipper, gulped it down. The waiter started away. Nick called him back.

"Send me the bartender!"

The bartender straightened his apron and came to the table. "Is anything wrong with the brandy, sir?" he asked.

Nick forced a smile. "Nothing. It is the best the Greeks can bottle. I wanted you here so that I can make an arrangement."

The bartender listened attentively.

"No one is to pay for a drink," he said, and emphasized in a louder voice, "a single drink while I am here."

The bartender's shoulders rose and fell, and he spread his hands in a gesture of not understanding. Nick made it clear.

"I wish to pay for all drinks. Any drinks. Any number of drinks that anyone wishes. Everything is on me." He gave the bartender a hundred dollar bill. "This is for you personally." Then he handed him a fistful, saying, "When this runs out let me know. Do you understand me?"

The bartender gathered in the bills. It was needless to count them. A hotel convention couldn't drink up that much in one evening.

"*Oui, Monsieur,* I understand perfectly," he said. "You are celebrating."

For a solid two months Nick stayed drunk, and during those two months no one was permitted to pay for a drink in any place he went in the city of Montreal. At the end of that period he sobered up enough for Jim and Max to put him on a train bound for Chicago.

By that time a safe bet would have been that there were not many bottles of Metaxas brandy left in the Canadian city.

Nick was never intoxicated again in his life.

Gambling Man

APOCRYPHAL sources, in trying to prove that gambling was an early addiction, have Nick flipping coins for oranges at age seven and being sent home from school to receive a spanking from his mother, accompanied by the warning, "You'll have to watch your step or you'll grow up to be a gambler."

To destroy such literary license, it might be pointed out that Crete, birthplace of Nicholas Andrea Dandolos, has thousands of orange trees; therefore one must draw the conclusion that a child had little to gain by winning a coin toss when all he had to do was reach up his hand and fill his stomach with the golden-skinned fruit.

Crete, anchored in the Mediterranean, is one of the five hundred Greek islands. Dwelling on its three thousand square miles are fewer than five hundred thousand inhabitants. In its stormy four thousand years of civilization Crete has known earthquakes, invasion, the Spanish painter El Greco, and Nick the Greek.

Nick, his parents, and baby sister Marie lived in the village of Rethímnon. His father, Andrea Dandolos, sold rugs. The family was much better off financially than many contemporaries who tried to scratch out a living from the rocky soil and raise small herds of goats and sheep. In some of the neighboring houses the livestock occupied the first floor of a dirt-floored dwelling, the people living on the second. It was an accepted way of life. Animals were the cherished possessions.

The women were the workhorses, responsible for the care of the family and the fields. The males lolled in the coffee houses, playing cards and backgammon, discussing politics, while drinking coffee or sipping ouzo, an anise-flavored liquor, but nonetheless were lords and masters of their households, the wives and children relegated to the roles of servants.

It was amidst such surroundings that the man who was to become a living legend—the icy, emotionless, highest-rolling gambler in the history of the world—was born.

He was always rather vague about his childhood. Writers of such stature as Mark Hellinger, Bob Considine, and Gene Fowler were among those who failed to dredge up his early memories. Besides this trio, any number of New York publishers and motion picture producers approached Nick for the purpose of securing his life story for a book. A smattering of the dialogue between Nick and these gentlemen of the hardcover houses went something like this:

PUBLISHER: Have you ever put down any of your life on paper?

NICK: The longest piece of writing I ever did is an eleven-word telegram. One word over the usual rate limit to prove I wasn't cheap, and not more than eleven words because you can't be too ungrammatical in such abbreviated writing.

PUBLISHER: Wouldn't you like to tell everything?

NICK: I'd violate too many trusts.

PUBLISHER: You might have a bestseller.

NICK: I'd have a subpoena.

PUBLISHER: You'd live forever in the public libraries.

NICK: It's rather dusty, dull, and drafty in there at night.

PUBLISHER: Do you think that success is a gamble?

NICK: Decidedly not. Business is not dependent on luck.

PUBLISHER: How much money do you estimate to have won and lost gambling?

NICK: I've never kept track. Magazine writers claim the amount is five hundred million dollars.

The one event Nick did recall clearly from his childhood, retelling the story in Nibbler's Restaurant in Beverly Hills, California, a month before he died, was what happened when he was five years old and his father brought home a lamb.

"Weighs about eighteen pounds," he heard the elder Dandolos inform his mother.

The lamb became his constant companion. Nick named her Manari, because Manari was the one lamb in every flock that the shepherds made a pet. Like the American dogs or cats, this lamb enjoyed full freedom of the house. Manari followed young Nick to school, waiting patiently until he left the crumbling, old stone building. Upon seeing him, Manari would bleat happily, and Nick, throwing his arms around the animal's fluffy neck, would run with her down the winding path.

She was the joy of his life.

When his teacher told the children that as they grew older they would learn the importance of Greek history, Nick showed little interest in the past. He was living only for the present. And Manari *was* his present.

Easter morning his mother woke him early and dressed him in his best clothes. Friends were coming for the Easter feast. When they arrived everyone talked and laughed a lot, and drank much tsichoudia (like ouzo, but stronger). They kept calling him Little Nicky.

Then they sat down at the table.

Bringing the meat from the kitchen on a huge platter, his mother set it before his father, as the man of the house always did the carving. He began sharpening the long knife on a whetstone he kept under the table. Nick used to love watching him hone the steel blade to a sharp edge and listening to the sound of it sliding over the stone surface.

"What a beautiful lamb!" one of the guests commented.

Suddenly Nick sensed something was wrong. He felt queasy, his forehead dampened, and when he swallowed there was a lump in his throat. He looked at his mother, who quickly turned her head away.

"Mama!" he cried. "Is it Manari?"

His father laid the knife down and said, "Nicholas, it is a Greek tradition to eat a baby lamb on Easter."

Again the boy's eyes sought his mother's.

"Is it Manari?"

This time his mother answered gently, "Yes, my son."

Jumping up, Nick ran from the table, upsetting his chair, and out of the house, scrambling up the flower-flecked hills through brilliant anemones, daisies, bell-flowers, camomiles, to a promontory where below him the wine-dark sea stretched to the horizon.

Here the soil was brown and barren and windswept. He lay with his head against a rock, and little rivers of tears slid down into the corners of his mouth. For the first time he actually tasted them; he'd always heard they were salty, but to him they were bitter—the way he felt toward his parents.

From that day on he couldn't eat lamb without vomiting.

In addition to the lamb episode and his education, little else could be pried from Nick about his childhood. Of Crete he would say, "Crete has a gnarled face, and some day I'd like to go back and travel on foot over her wrinkles."

He always referred to Crete as "she."

Nick hadn't wanted to become a gambler any more than he wanted to sell wholesale figs. Philosophy had been his life. To understand Nick it is necessary to understand Socrates (469–399 B.C.), whose teachings were preserved in the writings of Plato, Aristotle, and Xenophon. Socrates, acclaimed as the founder of Western philosophy, maintained that his sole wisdom consisted in recognizing his complete ignorance. He drank poison hemlock after being condemned to death by Athenian rulers who accused him of leading youth into false paths.

"We have men today who are accused of the same thing," Nick maintained, "but shrewd lawyers get them off scot-free."

Originally Nick became a gambler because it was a commercial shortcut to winning the girl he loved. He was forced into this position without choice, by circumstances more than fate. He shrugged it off philosophically. "What must be shall be," he said. He knew that he wasn't an habitual or a compulsive gambler. He didn't want to win merely for the sake of recording a triumph—something the psychoanalysts call "infantile megalomania," meaning the man holding the cards or throwing the dice has regressed to infancy. Gambling gave him no orgiastic pleasure. No psychic masochism was involved. Definitely, he was no pathological gambler.

Then why, he asked himself, am I gambling?

He offered three reasons:

1. The thrill. He compared gambling to a trout fisherman catching fish, not for eating purposes, but merely for the thrill of the catch—a contest pitting man against a wary, smart piscatorial creature.

2. It permitted him to lead a better life. Not for material gain, for externals meant next to nothing to him; but it opened the doors wide for introductions to intelligent and colorful people who provided an escape from ennui.

3. Charity. He was able to distribute huge sums of money to the needy in the role of a one-man relief agency. Reliable sources vouch for him having given away five million dollars to individuals he believed deserving of help, having put more than thirty youths through college, having started three hun-

dred fifty people in business, and having donated anonymously to organized charity.

Then there were the day-to-day handouts to grifters, moochers, con men, and a small number with legitimate reasons for needing financial help. Many of these people lined up in front of his hotel room door, waiting, sometimes for hours, until he appeared. Admitting them singly, he would listen to their hard luck stories and generally give them sums of from ten to a thousand dollars, the amount dependent on how convincing were their words. A flow of tears usually meant an extra fifty.

His mail at times was enormous. All the letters requested money. Many of these pleading missives were addressed just: Nick the Greek, Las Vegas, Nevada. Some of these were ignored; for others he stuffed bills wrapped in a piece of newspaper into a hotel envelope, with no return address.

He never had a checking account, and even disliked cashing checks. Cash was always his way of life.

Nick took a room at the Palmer House. He felt no snobbishness toward Blue Island, frequently returned for visits, and his move was not motivated by desire to seek a tonier atmosphere; the Palmer House was simply located closer to the big action in poker and dice. Each evening found him faultlessly attired in evening clothes, even if he dined alone in his room.

In 1871 the Great Chicago Fire had leveled the hotel owned by Potter Palmer, together with ninety-five buildings whose tenants paid him rent. The social leader was practically wiped out financially. In fact, he lacked enough money to pay the taxes on his scorched ground. Palmer promptly borrowed $1,700,000 from the insurance company. No security was necessary. Only his signature and good intentions.

The new Palmer House claimed to be fireproof, and one of

the hotel features was the barber shop where silver dollars were imbedded in the floor. It was here that Nick was shaved daily and sometimes manicured.

On one occasion when a manicurist accidentally stabbed him with a scissors, Nick cut short the young lady's apologies by remarking, "A man is lucky to lose only a single drop of blood on the field of combat."

It has been said that every young man has a hero from whom he draws personal inspiration, be he an athletic god, a captain of industry, a history maker, or an outstanding liberal. Nick had his idol, too. The difference was that the man he most admired entered his life belatedly after his return to Chicago.

"Everybody should have a hero," Nick said many years ago. "You have to chase a hero like a dream, worshiping from afar, but it is wise never to catch up to him and reach the introduction stage. Should this happen, it dawns upon you that your hero is made of flesh and bone and has fears and complexes like the average man; *ergo*, the idol is shattered."

Nick never caught up with his ideal: Richard Albert Canfield, 1855-1914. Historians list him as an American gambler and the inventor of the game solitaire. Historians are often limited to short summaries. Canfield stood for much more than "gambler" and card-game "inventor."

Nick became a collector of Canfield lore, questioning every person with whom he came into contact who claimed a friendship with or knowledge of the man. His admiration for Canfield centered around the monetary risks he took, his *savoir-faire*, and the fact that he was a self-educated gentleman. His Club House, a combination restaurant and gambling casino in Saratoga, famous New York State spa, became world renowned. There the man cognomenized "Prince of Gamblers" entertained such distinguished figures as Diamond Jim Brady, Lillian Russell, Louise Montagne, John Philip Sousa, Schumann-Heink, Chauncey Olcott, De Wolf Hopper, John

Drew, Anna Held, the Whitneys, the Vanderbilts, J. Pierpont Morgan, Florenz Ziegfeld, Victor Herbert, and many others.

After 1907 Saratoga boasted of the same curative waters, the same racetrack, the same two block-long hotels: the United States and the Grand Union; but somehow the illustrious resort lost something in status after the closing that year by reformers of the Canfield enterprise.

In the flourishing days of Richard Canfield the northern New York watering grounds was a mini-world of compressed pleasures, frequented by the socially elite and titled from Europe. The Gay Nineties were never gayer than at this popular and expensive summer resort. Many preferred it to anything offered abroad. During the lush years—seventeen, all told— nearly every millionaire in America hardy enough to travel paid Saratoga a visit.

Squarely into the vortex of this social whirl stepped Canfield, a former New England hotel night clerk who had used his long hours of inactivity to supplement his paltry formal education by reading everything he could lay his hands on. Later he became co-operator of a faro game that the law caught up with, and a judge sentenced him to six months in prison. Instead of crossing off the days on the calendar, Canfield took advantage of his incarceration to haunt the prison library.

Upon his release he headed for New York City, where he opened a gaming club catering to faro, poker, and roulette. Two years of fashionable patrons made him a millionaire, but the acquisition of a fortune failed to still his ambitions. In 1893 he bought the Saratoga Club House for $250,000.

He promptly imported a Paris chef and charged outrageous prices, higher than Sherry's or Delmonico's in New York City. Evening clothes were obligatory.

Then he did two things that brought hosannas from Nick: he extended liberal credit to those with good ratings, and on request, raised the betting limit. Maximum chip was of brown color and worth $100,000. Blue was the lowliest, valued at only $10.

The *New York World*, published by Joseph Pulitzer, dispatched its sensation-seeking star reporter, Nelly Bly, to comb Saratoga for feature stories. One, titled "The Monte Carlo of America," had as the lead paragraph:

This town has gone mad with the mania of gambling. From the Carlsbad of America, Saratoga has become its Monte Carlo—a Monte Carlo with the reckless law breaking of Leadville, Colorado, combined with the vulgarity of the Bowery.

Especially approved by Nick was the fact that Canfield was a loner. He had no partners, no backers. He alone was responsible for success or failure. His personal income rocketed to nearly $12 million. Every year his interest in paintings and rare book editions took him to Europe, where he made extensive purchases.

Rather than encourage big bettors such as Freddy Hostetter, reckless spending young millionaire, a $200,000 loser, to try for a comeback, he invited them to his private office for a bottle of vintage champagne and a short lecture, the theme of which was not to try to recoup their losses, predicting they would "just get in deeper."

Few took his fatherly counsel.

Canfield's highest rolling guest was John Warne "Bet-a-Million" Gates. Gates set a record for Saratoga betting one day by dropping $400,000 at the track, another $150,000 at faro, and then staging a turn-around so that at the end of play he was out only $250,000. Silver and copper mining kings took comparable thrashings.

Canfield was of the opinion that gambling was the greatest temptation in a man's life, and a quotation of his that Nick always recalled was: "They gambled in the Garden of Eden, and they will again if there's another one."

Canfield dropped millions in a stock market crash, but

nevertheless died a few hundred thousand dollars short of having a million left. His death occurred not long after he sat for James Abbott McNeill Whistler for a portrait that was never finished due to the painter's death.

Of course Nick and Canfield were in opposite gambling camps: one siding with the house, the other against it. But they were linked by a common bond: nerve. Nick summed up Canfield by declaring, "He had intelligence and breeding and daring, which are more important than a royal flush or throwing a seven or eleven. Canfield was the last of a vanishing breed —the individual gambling house operator. After him the syndicates took over."

Temporarily abandoning horse racing, Nick began heavy traffic in other gambling games. He could get all the action he wanted in the Loop. At the drop of a suggestion he was ready to play any game at any time. Within the space of a few weeks, during which he had taken sporadic trouncings at faro, craps, roulette, poker, and twenty-one (blackjack), he began zealously to study these pastimes in much the manner he had horse racing, and came to some conclusions: roulette and twenty-one were not for him. The thrill wasn't there, and the percentage against winning was too high.

He had a vendetta against all slot machines. To him they were something to be avoided like a plague. "Greedy metal monsters," he called them, "whose maws seem bottomless. In order to win a player shouldn't use coins, only a screwdriver."

Nick often played at a private casino, the Hoffman Club. Here, in his personal humidor, he stored his specially made Cuban cigars, strong and long. They cost him $1.50 each. During lengthy gambling sessions he was seldom without one in his mouth, a chainsmoker burning up as many as thirty per day and chewing each stub meditatively. He would place the cigar box in a spot close to the action, leaving the lid open for anyone to help himself. His cigar bill was estimated to be $700 monthly.

Certain that his parents would discover he was no longer in the fig business (from friends of theirs in Blue Island), he wrote that he was now in shipping. "Shipping" was a rather obscure kind of business that could range over a wide area, from the Chicago River to Lake Michigan to the oceans, and was not easily traceable.

He sent his parents $20,000. They were astounded by the vast sum. "People have always said that America is a land of opportunity," the elder Dandolos remarked to his wife, "but I didn't believe them until now."

"It's a shame," Mrs. Dandolos said enigmatically.

"What's a shame?" her husband inquired.

"That our son Nicholas isn't married." She pointed a finger at her husband. "You must do something about it. It is your duty as head of the House of Dandolos."

"How?"

"You go to America," she advised, "to this city of Chicago, the Blue Island part, visit, and find him a nice wife."

Mr. Dandolos protested, but finally consented to travel. He arrived in Chicago, a large, formidable-looking man with a wide, bushy moustache, speaking no English. Nick quartered him in an adjoining room at the Palmer House.

"Show me your shipping office," was his initial request.

Nick took him in a taxi, and in the middle of the business district pointed to a building. "That's the place."

"Stop the car!" ordered the senior Dandolos. "I'll get out and look it over."

"You can't," Nick hastily replied.

Mr. Dandolos twisted the corners of his moustache, puzzled. "Why can't I?"

"Closed on Wednesdays," Nick said, furnishing no further explanation.

"I understand," Mr. Dandolos said. "Then take me to Blue Island, the place where all the Greeks live."

Nick gave the driver a street address in the center of the

settlement. He had meant to take his father for a short stroll, intending to be careful not to introduce him to any shady characters he might know. But the moment his father stepped from the taxi he called, "See you tonight for dinner," and disappeared down the street.

Nick went into a restaurant and ordered a chicken sandwich and a glass of milk. When he finished and walked out, a shoeshine boy ran up to him.

"You Nick the Greek, mister?"

Nick admitted that he was.

"Can I have your autograph?" the boy asked, eyes widening as he stepped back to sweep Nick with an admiring look.

"No," Nick snapped, the mere thought of signing anything making him jittery.

Before Nick could walk away, the boy proposed, "Match you for a dime, Mr. Nick."

Nick dug out a coin, tossed it into the air, caught it deftly and clamped it concealingly against the back of his wrist.

"Call it!"

"Heads," the boy chose.

Lifting his fingers slightly, Nick took a peek. It was tails. He handed the ten cent piece to the boy. "You win," he acknowledged. "Now you can say you beat Nick the Greek."

The boy looked at the dime reverently, caressing it as if it were a rare collector's item.

"I'm gonna frame it," he said.

"Good," Nick replied, adding, "and let's hope you never have to spend it."

The elder Dandolos met his son for dinner. He refused to give a specific answer as to his activities of the day. All he said was, "I'm working on something."

Nick hadn't the slightest idea of what the mysterious "something" might be. He sought out a friend, George Pappas, who spoke Greek fluently. He hired George for twenty dollars a day, plus expenses, to escort his father around the city and point out the sights. He was to report to Nick at the end of each day.

From the first accounting of how his father spent the hours of the day, Nick gleaned little. "All he wants to do is call on people in Blue Island," Pappas revealed.

Nick asked why.

"Why? Is a good question," Pappas returned. "I drive him around and he talks very little. He keeps gazing out the window, and when he sees a nice house with a well-kept yard he tells me to stop. Then he goes in. I don't know what for." Pappas threw up his hands in despair.

Nick was soon to discover the reason for the peregrinations of his parent. Chris, who could pick up a Blue Island rumor at birth, telephoned him. Nick couldn't believe his ears. It seems that his father was a dedicated man bent on a mission: to find a suitable wife for him. At random he was picking the occupants of neat-appearing houses, on the chance that an unmarried daughter lived there who was seeking a husband. Then a sales pitch would be given to the mother of the girl by the elder Dandolos on behalf of his son.

Incredible, Nick thought, trying to remember if this were an Old Country tradition. Wondering what his father said about him, he asked Chris. The answer was slightly shocking.

Chris said, "Your father, in mentioning your excellent husband qualities, stressed the fact you saved every penny, had a fine, steady job, and that you were extremely cautious, never taking a chance on anything."

Nick hung up and mopped his brow.

The elder Dandolos burst into the room that evening with the jubilant announcement, "My boy, you're engaged to be married!"

Nick's cigar nearly dropped from his mouth.

"To whom, may I ask?"

"Her name is Persephone Kyriacou. Her father owns a restaurant. They make a wonderful Baklava [a Greek pastry of many paper-thin sheets of dough, blanched almonds, honey and sugar]. Very tasty," he said enthusiastically, smacking his lips.

"I am happy to learn about the Baklava," Nick said, "but if you don't mind, will you please describe the woman I am to wed?"

Mr. Dandolos twirled this handsome moustache. "Let me see now," he said, lost in thought. "Her hip bones are well covered, and her stomach shows she has been raised on good food. She . . ."

"You are trying to tell me she is fat, aren't you?" Nick guessed.

Mr. Dandolos frowned. "Well . . . now . . . Nicholas," he began slowly, "she has no excessive weight that a diet would not take off, and . . ."

"Father," Nick interrupted, "you wish me to believe that a fat Greek girl whose father owns a restaurant with all that Baklava handy can lose weight?"

"If she puts her mind to it," Mr. Dandolos stubbornly argued.

Nick smiled and said, "You don't know women very well." Then, becoming deadly serious and truthful, he made a clean breast of his life, acquainting his father with the fact that he was unemployed, that he was a gambler, and that he found life satisfactory.

The elder Dandolos was momentarily stunned by the disclosure. To him gamblers were of the same ilk as forgers, burglars, murderers. He sank into a chair, burying his face in his hands, moaning, "My son . . . my son . . ." Then he bounced to his feet, his grief apparently over, and asked Nick to get him a certain telephone number. Reaching it, Nick handed the telephone to his father.

"Mr. Kyriacou," the elder Dandolos said, his voice disappointment-choked, "I regret to inform you that the engagement between my son and your daughter is hereby called off."

He hung up.

After another week in Chicago Mr. Dandolos returned to Greece; but before departing he had a fatherly talk with his son, expressing a fervent hope that he would mend his errant ways and seek honorable employment—preferably in the restaurant business, even if it meant starting as a waiter. By diligently applying himself, he prophesied, his son might some day own the establishment.

Nick patted him on the back, shoved a wad of bills into his coat pocket, and told him not to worry. "You tried your level best," he said, referring to his short engagement period, "and you nearly had me living off the fat of the land."

Nick's reputation as a free-lance gambler was growing to giant proportions—yet he was barely aware of it. Chris tried to convince him. "You're the hottest thing since the Chicago fire," he said.

A few nights later, in an Italian-Greek club, Nick inadvertently had his reputation put to a test. He sat down in a stud poker game and bought $10,000 worth of chips. Six players circled the green felt surface of the table. Nick knew five of them well. The one he didn't know was heavyset, bull-necked, deep in his seventies. No one introduced them, as it was assumed they had already met. The next day the older man remarked, "At first I had no idea who he was. I thought he was some rich man's son."

Nick won a little, lost a little. Finally there was a juicy pot, and Nick and the old man were bucking heads; the rest had dropped out. Nick had a king in the hole, with a jack, eight, and nine showing. His opponent had an ace in the hole, with a queen, six, eight, and ten up. There was about $16,000 in the pot as they came to the last card. Nick drew a deuce and the old man pulled a four.

The old man bet, pushing in $4,400 worth of chips. Nick realized that he was beaten and had no intention of calling. Just as he was about to fold his cards and acknowledge defeat, a friend of his approached, hailing him with "Hello, Nick."

The old man squinted across the table at Nick. Then he nudged the player next to him and whispered, "Nick who?"

"Why, Nick Dandolos," was the reply.

The old man's face paled. "You . . . you mean Nick the Greek?" he sputtered.

"Sure," the other player said, "I thought you knew him."

Nick had been studying the old man and picking up the conversation. He noticed he was visibly shaken. Slowly Nick counted his pile of chips. In front of him was $11,828. Shoving the mountain of chips into the center of the table, he said evenly, "Call you and raise you $7,428."

The old man's hand shook and his voice trembled as he again whispered to the player alongside of him, "You sure he's Nick the Greek?"

"Of course. Ask anybody here."

The old man doubled up his fist and smashed it into the palm of the other hand as he made a decision. "You win," he said to Nick, getting up and leaving the table.

Nick pulled in the pile of chips.

As he sipped a brandy after the game ended, an acquaintance, trying to make conversation, asked if he ever resented being called Nick the Greek.

Lowering the brandy snifter, Nick replied, as he swirled the liquor around, "Sometimes it has its advantages."

That same evening, looking for more action, Nick dropped in on a dice game on Halsted Street, run by Negroes although the majority of players were Caucasians. Here the house managed the game, taking a very small cut from each shooter. It was the players themselves who covered the bets.

Nick had barely shouldered his way up to the table when it was his turn to handle the dice. He never cared especially for rolling the dice himself. His preference was to play the "don't pass" line, taking the odds. A national magazine once dubbed him the "Aristotle of the don't pass line."

He did not subscribe to the theory that a shooter can feel the dice growing hot and that that is the time to push his luck, passing the cubes to the next player when the feeling subsides.

"That's sheer nonsense," Nick contended. "The dice don't know who's throwing them. They can't be controlled telepathically. A three-year-old child can throw them as well as a top gambler."

That was why on this evening Nick, backing up his logic, placed only a two dollar bet on the pass line. Suddenly he was streaking. He couldn't miss. He let the money ride through seventeen straight passes, until there was $294,144 in cash on the table. He had thrown the dice lackadaisically, as if indifferent to what point came up, minus any of the customary loud exhortations.

"Let it ride," he said.

There were no takers.

He stuffed the money into every pocket and left, heedless of any possible heists.

All this had happened too fast. It was not yet midnight—to Nick, a long time until the shank of the evening. Going to bed was unthinkable. Hopping into a cab, he headed for Blue Island, hoping to find a wizened old Greek street peddler named Petro Alerou in a coffee house he frequented. He was the champion backgammon player of Blue Island—perhaps, in the opinion of many, of the entire world.

Alerou's face lighted up as he saw Nick making his way toward him. This Dandolos was a tough adversary, one of the few who had ever bested him. "You wish to play me?" he asked hopefully.

"It will be an honor," Nick said.

"Same stakes."

"Agreed."

Alerou asked solicitously, "It will not hurt you financially if you are defeated?"

"No," Nick said, hanging up his overcoat and sitting down at the table.

The ancient Greek opened the double board, dropping the dice in the cardboard cup, rattling them noisily. A crowd was forming behind the table. Some individual betting was going on.

At the end of three hours Nick had suffered a crushing defeat. He paid Alerou, thanked him for the game, and taxied to the Palmer House.

He had lost $8.80.

Glancing at the lobby clock he noted it was nearly 5:00 A.M. Rather reluctantly he pressed the elevator button, got off at his floor, and went to bed.

A Present from Al Capone

W HEN Nick delved into the history of dice, he was
delightfully surprised to discover that one of the
earliest traceable mentions came from a countryman
of his, Sophocles, who ascribed their invention to Palamedes.
Palamedes had no foresight, when he taught the Greeks how
to play during the siege of Troy, that frenetic segments of
future generations would detach themselves from the norm to
shout exhortations at these small cubes and call the game
"craps."

Early devotees of the game included Mark Antony and the
Emperors Augustus, Nero, and Claudius. Sporadic cheating is
said to have reared its ugly head during those early periods in
history.

It amused Nick that he was credited by writers for elevat-
ing the game of dice from down-on-the-knees in dirty alleys
to plush palaces. "I only helped lift it to its former pinnacle,"
he said. "During its inception it was a game for royalty before
the commoners acquired a taste for the fast action."

He was particularly fond of a quotation from Virgil that
characterized the spirit of the age a quarter of a century before the coming of Christ:

What ho! Bring dice and good wine
Who cares for the morrow?
Live—so calls grinning death—
Live, for I come to you soon.

The era of unrestrained gambling in Chicago in which Nick participated flourished under the rein of Mayor "Big Bill" Thompson. For an unbroken string of years—1872 to 1931—ganglords ruled the city's vice and gambling, namely: Mike McDonald, Dion O'Banion, Big Jim Colosimo, Johnny Torrio, and Al Capone. Killers for hire were cheap, plentiful, and accurate, as evidenced by the St. Valentine's Day Massacre, an event unsurpassed for pure bloodletting in hoodlum history.

With the exception of the early-day Mike McDonald, Nick knew them all and enjoyed their confidences. He gambled and entertained at their respective temples of pleasure. They passed along the word to their contemporaries in the Eastern rackets that Nick was a "right guy," and he soon had standing invitations to look up Jack Legs Diamond and Dutch Schultz in New York City.

It was Dutch Schultz who was to pay him the zenith of compliments when he said, "That Nick is a man to be trusted. A dentist couldn't pry his mouth open."

Crap games were ubiquitous in those days, and the combined clickings of the dice rattling through the air like a telegrapher's key was an irresistible siren's call. Nick circulated from game to game, winning more than he dropped. His greatest pleasure was to walk into a game and offer to make a $50,000 wager on the coming out point, the takers being those around the table who would pool their resources to cover the bet. Then, win or lose, he would walk out, head for the next game, usually only a few blocks distant, and repeat this *modus operandi* throughout the night.

"This provides exercise," Nick explained. "Games played with any kind of ball are too violent for the body and stamp no character on the mind. As I walk from crap game to crap game, my brain becomes active and agile and dwells on lofty thoughts."

After a lucky night during which, pursuing these hit-and-miss or hit-and-score tactics, he picked up around $300,000 —the last bundle coming from a club operated by the omnipotent Al Capone—he was just about to climb into bed when there was a rap on the door and a voice called:

"Telegram for Mr. Dandolos."

Nick started for the door, then stopped dead in his tracks. In a hotel enjoying the reputation of the Palmer House such messages would be telephoned from the desk, if not held for a more respectable arising hour. Also, come to think of it, he had telephoned the switchboard that he wasn't to be disturbed until noon.

It sounded clear and simple, like a heist. He could have just called through the door for whoever was outside to go away, but that wouldn't have been very exciting. Besides, curiosity demanded that he know how many were out there. Tiptoeing across the sitting room and grasping the doorknob firmly, he jerked it open about four inches, saw three men he didn't recognize, and banged it shut before they could make a forced entrance.

"Go away, boys," he called through the door. "The game is over and the police are on the way."

Despite the thickness of the Palmer House carpets he could distinctly hear footsteps retreating down the corridor. The next afternoon he telephoned Al Capone and made an appointment for that same night.

Capone, of late, was receiving more newspaper coverage than a South American revolution. Only recently he had been brought in by police and accused of several underworld killings; but as usual, he had the same old reliable alibi—"I was in Cicero when that happened"—and there were a dozen witnesses attesting to having seen him there at that certain hour.

Nick had met Capone three or four times at the Colosimo Club and at the Ship, a Cicero gambling establishment owned by Torrio and O'Banion. His rise had been astronomical. Now, his reputation and empire burgeoning, he owned a dozen gambling and drinking clubs, and due to Prohibition, he prospered by brewing and distributing his own liquor.

Nick shot crap for an hour and then asked to see Capone. He was ushered into his private office, where he told the underworld lord of the abortive heist. Capone angrily pounded on the desk with a closed fist, a sea of papers dancing from the impact.

"My customers have gotta be protected," he roared. "They ain't gonna get away with it."

He pushed a buzzer. Several of his tough boys came in. Capone gave them a capsule account of what had happened to Nick, and said, "Find out who tried to pull this, and bring 'em in."

Nick started to rise from his chair, but Capone asked him to sit down, scowled, and said, "These were cheap punks that tried to heist you, Nick. My boys will run this down fast and I'll take care of 'em." He scratched at his receding hairline. "Now seriously, Nick, you carry around too much money on dark streets and I know you never pack a rod. Ain't you afraid?"

"Fear is more painful to cowardice than death to true courage," Nick answered.

"Huh?" Capone said.

"I'm not afraid, Al, but it's somewhat of a nuisance, and you can't tell when one of these boys has nervous fingers."

Capone agreed. "Some of them might. We wanta protect our customers—particularly good ones like you—so you're sure to get home with what you won. Why, a man like you is a regular walking bank."

"You don't have to worry about me tonight," Nick said, mentioning that he had dropped around $18,000.

Capone wasn't listening. "I could give you a card like I gave Harry Richman," he mused, referring to the popular musical comedy star. "Harry got held up just the other night as he started to get into a cab. As they took his wallet, Harry said to one of the two stickup guys, 'Take a good look at the card inside.' He did, and it said: 'Please lay off the bearer of this card, Harry Richman, or you'll have me to account to. Al Capone.'

"They give him back the wallet and beat it down the street," Capone concluded.

Nick declined. "Thanks, but I don't want a card. I'd forget to carry it."

Capone made a sudden decision. "I'll tell you what I'll do, Nick. Tomorrow I'm sendin' you Honest John. A present from me. He'll give you personal protection. John's one of the best in the business."

"Best what?" Nick inquired.

"Best shots."

Nick thanked Capone politely and said he didn't want a bodyguard.

At noon the following day, Nick, clad in blue-and-cream-colored striped pajamas, answered a knock on his door. A glum-faced, expressionless man, attired in a dark suit with heavily padded shoulders, announced, "I'm Honest John, your new bodyguard."

"I don't want one, thanks," Nick returned, starting to close the door. A size-twelve shoe got in the way. Honest John stepped into the room.

"You got one anyway," he said. "Boss's orders."

Nick whistled resignedly. "To appreciate heaven, you have to have a few days of hell," he mumbled, telephoning room service and asking his new bodyguard, "How do you like your eggs, John?"

"Over easy."

Nick bathed and dressed. Honest John, the triggerman, followed every move he made, eyes glued on him. With the exception of his opening remarks upon gaining entrance to the room and mentioning his preference in eggs, he hadn't uttered a single word.

Nick interrogated him. "What's your education, Mr. John?"

No answer.

"How long have you been associated with Mr. Capone?"

No answer.

"Are you familiar with philosophy?"

No answer.

"Have you ever read a book?"

No answer.

"What is your prime purpose of life?"

Honest John brightened, flashed a gold-toothed grin. He seemed to like the question because it wasn't too personal.

"To kill people," he said, smiling.

"Don't you know," Nick informed him, "that violence begets violence?"

A knock sounded. In two quick, pantherish strides Honest John reached the door.

"Come in," Nick called. The door was unlocked.

Chris entered.

Honest John leaped at the visitor, twisted his right arm behind his back, cautioning, "Don't move." Locked in that tight vise, Chris couldn't have moved if his life depended on it. Honest John frisked him and turned to Nick. "He's clean," he said, releasing his prisoner.

Chris frowned, gently massaging his arm. Nick apologized. "My unwanted bodyguard," he disclosed. "He has an uncurbed predilection for violence."

Nick had an engagement that evening with a chorus girl dancing in a musical revue. As he finished dressing for the occasion, he saw that his worst fears were about to be realized: Honest John was going along.

John had his reasons. "She might be a decoy leadin' ya into a trap," he said dramatically.

"Huh!" Nick snorted, "You've been seeing too many gangster movies."

Try as he might, Nick couldn't shake the faithful Honest John. The two of them waited in a taxi near the stage door exit. The girl—whose name was Betty—a natural blonde, came out clad in a bulky pseudo-fur coat. Nick waved and called her name. She hopped in, leaned forward to embrace him, and found herself slammed into the seat with the hands of Honest John reaching under her coat, running the length of her body.

She screamed.

The cab driver swung around. "No rough stuff, please, gents."

Nick said soothingly, "Don't be alarmed, my dear, he is simply frisking you."

"That's a new word for it," Betty said, visibly shaken.

After three days of Honest John's constant companionship and watchful vigilance, Nick's calm exterior began to show chinks of cracking up. The bodyguard slept in his sitting room, stood sentry duty outside his bathroom door, and once grabbed Nick's plate of steak away before he was able to taste a piece.

"Just who do you think is plotting to poison me?" Nick asked exasperatedly as Honest John began chewing reflectively on the steak.

"Some cook with a grudge."

Nick sighed. "I don't know any cooks, with or without grudges." He held out his hand. "Now, if you will kindly give me back my dinner."

Honest John passed over the steak with one bite missing.

That same evening the Coal Miner telephoned. Nick talked with him while Honest John stood with an ear cocked toward the receiver, trying vainly to overhear the conversation. The Coal Miner, so cognomenized because he once dug coal in Pennsylvania, was stud poker crazy, a wild, unpredictable player who had cleaned many gamblers of their bankrolls.

He challenged Nick to a two-handed game.

Two-handed poker was Nick's forte, a head-to-head clash of wits, skill, and daring. Of course, the hands weren't as good with so few cards dealt, but to Nick that was what made it interesting. In such a two-handed contest he had only to concentrate on, and read, one face. With a veteran cardplayer, face reading is sometimes valueless. If he wants to, the veteran dons a mask of inscrutableness. He is also part actor. He may groan if he has a flush, and grin delightedly on a pair of eights. Nick could usually tune in on these routines and be prepared when they were switched.

The Coal Miner came up to Nick's room, and after an introduction to Honest John, reached into his pockets and threw several red-backed decks on the table.

"These all right" he questioned, "or do you want to send out for some?"

"They'll do," Nick said.

By midnight Nick was a few thousand ahead. It had been, up to then, a pretty even game. Honest John sat behind the Coal Miner, his eyes riveted on him. The Coal Miner was a heavyset, florid-faced individual in his mid-forties, who perspired freely regardless of the temperature. Globules of sweat always gathered in the same patch on his forehead. Periodically he dragged out a colored handkerchief, mopped his brow, and about once hourly blew on his eyeglasses before carefully wiping them.

Nick played with his coat on. At all times he was fresh as if he had just finished twelve hours' sleep. One of his recent victims had described him as a guy sitting "with an icicle up his ass."

The Coal Miner paused as he gathered up the cards to shuffle. "I've got a rough day tomorrow," he said, "and I'd like to set a time limit."

"Name it."

"Let's see . . ." The Coal Miner tilted his head back, lost in thought. Then he looked at Nick. "Will six A.M. be satisfactory?"

Nick had no objection.

The Coal Miner dragged out a heavy-cased gold watch and snapped open the thick case, lying it on the table. Six hours later he consulted the timepiece and said, "I guess it's quittin' time."

They settled up. Nick handed the Coal Miner $39,000 and thanked him for the game. The Coal Miner went into the bathroom, and while he was gone Nick reached for the spread-out cards and dropped a queen of diamonds into his pocket. The Coal Miner returned, scooped up the cards, stacked them neatly, and pocketed them along with two other decks they had used.

He bade them goodnight.

For a long time after the Coal Miner had gone, Nick examined the queen of diamonds, microscopically going over every fraction of an inch on the back. No markings were visible. He went to bed, and the next morning after breakfast he again studied the cards. Finally, shaking his head, he placed the queen carefully in a coat pocket and asked Honest John, "Did you notice anything different about the Coal Miner's glasses?"

The answer was "Nope."

"The lenses?"

"Nope."

"That the glass wasn't clear?"

"Nope."

Nick said, "Well, they were tinted."

"What if they was?" Honest John inquired.

"I don't know exactly," Nick replied, "but I intend to find out." He tapped Honest John on the arm. "Come on, let's pay a visit to an acquaintance of mine."

They taxied to the industrial section of the city, stopping at a low, sprawling building housing a company that manufactured crooked gambling equipment: playing cards, roulette, and dice. The specialty of the house was "peeties," or "loaded blocks." These were dice heavily loaded with mercury.

The owner greeted Nick with surprise. "You here as a customer?" he wondered.

"No," Nick said, "I'm here to ask for your help."

"What can I do for you, Mr. Dandolos?"

Nick handed him the queen of diamonds. "Is this from one of your lines?"

After a cursory examination the manufacturer beamed. "Yes, it's our latest. Isn't it an undetectable beauty?"

"Possibly," Nick said, "but is it worth thirty-nine thousand dollars?"

"Hardly," the manufacturer said, shaking his head. "The deck—which comes in redbacks only—sells for ten dollars and the glasses for twenty-five."

"Glasses?"

"Oh, yes. Without them the deck is useless." The manufacturer opened a drawer and brought forth a pair of rose-tinted glasses, which he handed to Nick. Nick held them in the palm of his hand.

"Put them on."

Nick did. The manufacturer placed the queen of diamonds face down before him. "See anything unusual, Mr. Dandolos?"

Nick certainly could. Three dots. He took off the glasses.

"Nothing visible to the naked eye, eh?" grinned the manufacturer.

"Nothing. It's a work of genius."

The manufacturer rubbed his hands together greedily. "A

very satisfactory product," he said. "We have a heavy back-log of domestic and European orders. Yes," he repeated, "a very satisfactory product."

"Depending, of course, on who's wearing the glasses," Nick stated.

Suddenly it dawned on the manufacturer that Nick had been victimized. He apologized profusely and explained the mechanics of the cheating cards, which had to be red-backed, and the special glasses, known as "luminous readers."

Today such a form of cheating is elementary; any pair of glasses is suspect. But in those days they were an innovation.

When they were homeward bound, Nick said to Honest John, "I've got a job for you."

Honest John brightened, and his left hand reached under his coat to pat his shoulder holster. "When do I start work?"

Nick told him to be patient, that he had a plan which he would soon put into operation. In the meantime John was instructed to buy a good-quality rope and a bandana handkerchief. The next step was to arrange another card game with the Coal Miner. The Coal Miner was ready and eager.

In preparing for the arrival of the Coal Miner, the most important thing was gargling. Nick had done this on the hour throughout the day. It was a necessary precaution, but not against a cold or sore throat. He wished to insure the long duration of his golden-toned speaking voice.

The Coal Miner came in like a summer thunderstorm, greeting Nick and Honest John with booming hellos. He took off his coat and loosened his tie. The room temperature was around 70°, but the Coal Miner was wringing wet in the armpits, which showed plainly on his blue shirt. The big man tossed three packets of red-backed cards on the table, adjusted his glasses, and faced his host. "Ready, Nick?"

"I am, but I wonder if you are," Nick said softly.

The Coal Miner was confused. "I don't follow you."

Nick's voice hardened. "You will," he said, pointing to

Honest John. "May I call your attention to what my friend is holding in his hand."

Honest John was squinting down the barrel of a 7.63 mm. Mauser pistol using low-velocity ammunition. It was pointed at the Coal Miner.

"Now, wait a minute," the Coal Miner shrilled. "I—I . . ."

"The minute is up," Nick snapped. "Now go over and sit in that soft, comfortable chair," he ordered.

The Coal Miner did as told.

Nick went to him, jerked off his glasses, slit open one of the decks, and picked a card at random, after first putting on the tinted glasses. The markings on the back were plainly visible.

"It's a joke, Nick," the Coal Miner protested, his eyes darting from Nick to the gun held in the steady hand of Honest John. "It's only a joke, I was . . ."

"Pretty expensive and dangerous joke to play, wasn't it?"

The Coal Miner shifted his weight forward in the chair and started to reach toward his hip.

"Hold it, mister!" Honest John cried.

"But," the Coal Miner explained, settling back in the chair, "I was only going to give Nick his money back. That's what you want me to do, isn't it, Nick?" he said, twisting in the chair to stare at his host.

Nick waved his hand back and forth, a gesture to indicate he wasn't concerned, at the same time shaking his head and saying, "I don't want my money back. I rather enjoyed the game."

The Coal Miner was dumbfounded. "What do you want from me, then?" he asked, as if dreading the answer.

"You might call it revenge."

"But Nick . . ."

"Tie him up," Nick commanded, "and put the gag in his mouth."

Honest John moved fast. The Coal Miner spluttered protests, which were soon silenced by the bandana in his mouth.

He was bound fast to the chair. Perspiration dripped from his forehead. His eyes bugged with terror.

"You have a silencer on your gun?" Nick asked Honest John.

"Sure have," the bodyguard said happily. "Latest thing. Very quiet."

The Coal Miner rolled his eyes wildly, tried to twist his neck from side to side, and tugged at the secure bindings. His shirt looked as if he just stepped from a cloudburst.

Honest John peered at Nick, awaiting a signal. Anticipation showed on his face. "Now?" he asked.

"Put the gun away," Nick commanded.

"Please, Mr. Nick," Honest John begged.

"Put it away, John," Nick said sternly.

Reluctantly Honest John replaced the gun in its holster. He seemed ready to burst into tears.

"There'll be other chances," Nick placated.

A low moan came from the bodyguard as he sprawled dejectedly on the couch. His figure appeared collapsed and shrunken, a melancholy sight.

Nick moved to a position a few feet distant from his trussed-up visitor, and in a resonant voice began reciting from "Haidée" and "Don Juan," by Lord Byron:

> It was the cooling hour, just when the rounded
>   Red sun sinks down behind the azure hill,
> Which then seems as if the whole earth is bounded,
>   Circling all nature, hush'd, and dim, and still,
>
> With the far mountain-crescent half surrounded
>   On one side, and the deep sea calm and chill
> Upon the other, and the rosy sky,
>   With one star sparkling through it like an eye.

Walking slowly back and forth in front of the Coal Miner as he recited, and delivering the lines like a skilled thespian,

Nick exhausted his repertoire of Byron, then from the clear well of memory dredged up George Crabbe, William Blake, Samuel Rogers, Robert Bloomfield, and William Words-worth.

Nick took a five-minute recess, spending the time gargling in the bathroom. The Coal Miner sat quietly, breathing heavily, no longer straining at his bounds. His eyes had a glazed appearance and his face was a mask of boredom. Honest John crossed and uncrossed his legs restlessly.

Returning to the sitting room, Nick resumed his declamation. This time he began with Sir Walter Scott, went to Samuel Coleridge, Robert Southey, Walter Savage Lander, Thomas Campbell, John Galt, and concluded with James Leigh Hunt.

He took another break and again gargled. For two solid hours he had spouted poetry. The effect on his audience was telling. Honest John sat with his head in his hands, motionless. The Coal Miner's eyes begged for mercy.

But compassion was furthest from Nick's mind. Once again he launched into what seemed infinite verse, starting with Henry Kirke White and on to Thomas Love Peacock, Percy Bysshe Shelley, John Keble, Felicia Hemans, John Clare, John Keats, George Darley, and touching on Alfred, Lord Tennyson's "Mariana":

> With blackest mess the flower-pots
>   Were thickly crusted, one and all;
> The rusted nails fell from the knots
>   That held the pear to the gabled-wall.
> The broken sheds look'd sad and strange:
>   Unlifted was the clinking latch;
> Unweeded and worn the ancient thatch
>   Upon the lonely moated grange.
>
> She only said, "My life is dreary,
>   He cometh not," she said;

She said, "I am aweary, aweary,
I would that I were dead!"

Nick stopped and cleared his throat. "Enough, I believe," he decided in a low voice that showed a slight strain. "Untie him," he directed Honest John.

Honest John almost fell from the chair, limping perceptibly as he approached the Coal Miner. His foot had gone to sleep during the recitations, which had lasted nearly three hours. He undid the ropes, removed the gag.

The Coal Miner struggled to rise, but fell back into the chair gasping for air. Licking at his lips, he swallowed numerous times, attempting to stimulate the flow of saliva in his parched throat.

Nick asked him, "Did you learn anything from nineteenth-century English verse?"

The Coal Miner leaned forward, tried to speak, but no words came. At length he found his voice and said weakly, "Yes."

"What did you learn?"

"That last line," the Coal Miner recalled. "It was 'I would that I were dead!' Well, that's the way I feel."

Nick turned to Honest John. "And how do *you* feel? Did *you* learn anything?"

The bodyguard made a wry face. "I'm quittin', Mr. Nick. There's easier ways to make a buck."

"Goodnight, gentlemen," Nick said, heading for the bedroom.

They left together, and just before the door closed, words spoken by the Coal Miner to Honest John reached Nick: "If this ever happens again, just shoot me; it's more merciful."

When Nick got up the next morning he found a wad of bills piled up on an end table. He counted $39,000. His face broke into a quick smile as he thought that that was more money than all the poets whose works he'd recited ever made in a lifetime.

Ready for Rothstein

I N the 1920s, to establish herself in the social world, a girl
would brag, "I danced with the Prince of Wales." Edward,
Prince of Wales, known to the British Empire as "Prince
Charming," *bon vivant* and fashion precursor, did indeed
whirl many a panting maiden around ballroom floors; yet, to
have validated the preponderance of female dancing claims,
he would have needed as many feet as a centipede and the
stamina of a weightlifter.

During this same period, Nick the Greek, having departed
Chicago for other cities of sky's-the-limit gambling action,
found his own fame spreading until his name became a household one, and during lulls in conversations a voice might
claim, "The last time I played cards with Nick the
Greek . . ."

It was a toss-up whether more women were supposed to
have danced with the Prince or more men to have gambled
with Nick.

In 1925 Nick actually became acquainted with the Prince at
a party in New York given by Fanny Brice while she was
married to Nicky Arnstein. The next time they met was at the
Stardust Hotel in Las Vegas. Moe Dallitz, the owner, started

to introduce them, but found they already knew each other.

"I watched you play dice this evening," the Prince, who was now married and held the title of the Duke of Windsor, said, "and I certainly admire your nerve."

Nick said, "I think that on one occasion in your life you showed more nerve than I ever possessed." He was referring to the Duke having given up the throne for the love of the former Wally Simpson.

Just then the woman to whom he was alluding came over and linked her arm with her husband's. The Duke said to his wife, the Duchess, "My dear, I want you to meet the most famous man in the world."

They chatted for a few minutes, and the Duke's closing words to Nick were, "I hope you can visit us in Paris and, if possible, drop over to England and see my niece."

Thinking about it later, Nick came to the conclusion that everyone wanted to fix someone up with an ugly duckling member of the family. Then it suddenly dawned upon him. "My God!" he exclaimed to the emptiness of his hotel room. "That was the Queen of England he wanted me to meet."

In San Francisco, against a character known simply as Big Boy, Nick, in a game of lowball (worst hand wins: ace, two, three, four, five is the equivalent of a royal flush), won $1,200,000. It was a head-to-head struggle, and Big Boy's supporters—numbering twenty—all had a piece of the action.

The game was held in the Kingston Club.

Big Boy was a good loser. He had been outclassed and he knew it. He shook Nick's hand and suggested, "You ought to tangle with Arnold Rothstein."

At that time Rothstein, a New Yorker, was recognized as the King of Gamblers. It was inevitable that he and Nick would clash.

"I was gunning for him," Nick remembered. "I knew that some day there would be a showdown. It reminded me of the early American West, the Frontier days when a quick-draw artist was spoiling to cut another notch on his gun handle. I was out to get Arnold. It was a compulsion, I guess, an ego hangup and a reminder of something Christopher Morley once wrote:

> When ego, fantailed like a peacock,
> Can find the needle in the haycock
> And hold the needle's eye and thread it—
> Is that millennium? You said it!

Yes, someday, when ready, he was going to find Arnold Rothstein.

Handsome, striking, a dashing figure who gambled with shady characters and hobnobbed with socialites, Nick, playing like there was no tomorrow, left a trail of broken victims from San Francisco and Los Angeles to Detroit, New Orleans, and Hot Springs. Some of them never recovered. He made believers out of all. One of the defeated reminisced, "I got down on my knees to shoot craps with him, and I may never be able to get back on my feet again financially."

Columnists began writing of his spectacular exploits. Strangely enough, his losses more than his wins brought him publicity. Walter Winchell informed Mr. and Mrs. America and all the ships at sea about him. O. O. McIntyre frequently mentioned him in his column, as did Broadway columnist Mark Hellinger.

Nick deplored publicity. "It's the worst thing that can happen to you in my profession," he believed. "Too much of it can get you a one-to-ten-year jail sentence."

At a midnight charity show at Grauman's Chinese Theater in Hollywood attended by film luminaries, he received some unexpected notoriety. George Jessel, the toastmaster, after concluding introductions to Filmland's famous, called for silence. Then he said:

"And at this time, ladies and gentlemen, I wish to present a man who has a better claim to fame than nearly anybody here. Stand up, Nick the Greek!"

Embarrassed, Nick stumbled to his feet and quickly sat down again. The ovation was tumultuous. Not because of his gambling skills, but because he was known for his deeds of kindness in money handouts, which he tried to keep to himself, to out-of-work writers and actors.

"There's one advantage to being well-known," Nick once said. "It gives you an opportunity to meet colorful people who chase away bordeom. To these I owe an unpayable debt of gratitude."

When Nick first came to Los Angeles, he checked in at a downtown hotel, the Alexandria. As was customary, he took a single room. The Alexandria had an air of elegance, and this hostelry was the leading one in the city. Built in 1906, it added a new wing in 1916. The cocktail lounge was a popular rendezvous where deals—many of them motion picture—involving enormous sums of money were transacted.

Every day in the life of the Alexandria dozens of the famous walked across the lobby—President William Howard Taft, Franklin Delano Roosevelt, Mary Pickford, Roscoe "Fatty" Arbuckle, Jesse L. Lasky, and Cecil B. DeMille, to name only a handful. Nick knew them all.

He had no inkling as he sat in the Marathon Café, a Greek restaurant not far from his hotel, run by a countryman, Sperus Gielman, that as he was eating a dish of rizogalo a plot was hatching against him. It was a heist. But not an ordinary heist, and Nick was not the only intended victim. The heist was to be engineered by Herbert Emerson Wilson, who had resigned as pastor of the First Baptist Church in East San Diego, California, to embark on a career of crime.

Wilson, a talented, thinking type of criminal, an excellent organizer, was ahead of his time in efficiency methods. August Vollmer, former Berkeley, California, Chief of Police, had written of him:

"Herbert Emerson Wilson, with his syndicated crime methods, represented the highest peak that criminality has ever attained in this country or any other. No one, either before or since Wilson, has ever reached such a degree of criminal perfection."

This paragon of "criminal perfection," abetted by a hand-selected mob, was to enjoy five years of phenomenal accomplishments: sixty burglar-proof safes blasted or torched open and armored-car robberies pulled off from coat to coast for an aggregate loot of nearly $16 million.

Now, for a lark, a change of pace—and, of course, a contemplated measure of profit—Herbert Wilson was concentrating on Nick the Greek.

"It will be a feather in my cap to take the Greek," he told Jack Elwell, one of his crowd who first suggested robbing Nick.

Elwell was an expert "caser," a shrewd man of exact appraisals with a continental flair, an indisputably excellent con man who had the ability to spot a mark at long range. He radiated confidence. People had unshakable faith in him. Once Elwell's arm closed around an intended dupe's shoulders, the poor fellow was rendered helpless. Installed in an expensive suite at the Alexandria, he was—or so his business cards proclaimed—a man of varied interests. His portfolio included oil, gas, stocks, bonds, real estate. Just name a business, and Elwell could produce a card and conversation fitting it.

The work Elwell performed for Wilson did not entail too much personal risk. His job was to steer the boss to a prospective job. Then he would quietly back off, his work finished, and receive a share of the profits.

Elwell asked Wilson if he had ever heard of the notorious gambler Nick the Greek.

Wilson chuckled. "Who hasn't?" was his answer.

"What do you know about him?"

Wilson, reclining in one of the comfortable chairs in the

Elwell suite, thought a moment and answered, "He stands for big money. Real big. One of the highest rollers, I believe."

"He is *the* highest roller in the U. S. with the exception of Arnold Rothstein in the East."

"Well?" Wilson leaned back, half closed his eyes, and waited.

Elwell said with conviction, "I know Nick. Nick trusts me. Nick will go anywhere for a bigtime poker game. He's loaded. Made a killing in San Francisco. I . . ."

The telephone jangled.

"Excuse me, Herb," Elwell said, reaching for the instrument. He talked for half a minute about a board of directors' meeting in the morning, and hung up. "Where was I?" he asked.

"Telling me how much money Nick the Greek has," Wilson reminded.

"Oh, yes," Elwell recollected, picking up the story. "Well, I go out and invite some of the leading action boys for a game, Nick incuded. The game's held right here in my suite. I'll see to it that it's a cash game—no chips. There'll be a fortune on the table. And . . ."

"I walk in with some of the boys—masks on, of course— and sweep up what's on the table, what's in their pockets, and what's on their fingers."

"Exactly," Elwell agreed. "One more thing, though."

"Name it."

"So nobody suspects I'm in on it, someone better mess me up a little," he suggested.

Wilson nodded.

"But just a little," Elwell repeated.

Wilson rose to go.

"I'm a trifle ashamed of myself to have to pull this on a right guy like Nick the Greek," Elwell said with a trace of remorse.

Wilson shrugged. "It's a dog-eat-dog world," he reminded him.

"Thanks for justifying my role," Elwell said, relieved.

Wilson sat down again, and for fifteen minutes they discussed the *modus operandi*. It was a simple plan, fast and seemingly foolproof. And the victims-to-be were the sort who wouldn't file a complaint with the police.

Wilson got in touch with his henchmen. He lined up his brother Lou, George Redding, and Charlie Stahal. He was sure of his brother and Redding, almost sure of Stahal. Wilson abhorred violence and was continually preaching against it. Before he met Stahal he had heard rumors that the man—a toughie out of Chicago—was "trigger happy." But Wilson had coached him for a year and believed he had calmed him. To date, Stahal hadn't come close to squeezing a trigger.

Wilson also enlisted the aid of Marion Kildare, a beauty capable of prying a secret from the lips of an Egyptian mummy. In the past, bank officials had been her prey, and from them she gleaned important information which was passed along to Wilson. Her particular job in this latest operation was simply to sit in the lobby and, mentally armed with a description of the poker players, report if they had all gone upstairs.

At 11:15 P.M. Wilson and his brother entered the lobby of the Alexandria. George Redding sat scribbling at a writing desk. Charlie Stahal leaned against a marble column, puffing on a fat cigar. The girl signaled Wilson that the gamblers were upstairs.

Wilson and his brother walked into the elevator. Redding and Stahal followed, got off the floor below the Elwell suite, and climbed a flight of stairs to meet the others. They congregated before Elwell's door. Herbert Wilson was to wait outside and the others enter.

Lou Wilson, Redding, and Stahal slipped small rubber masks over their faces and took out their revolvers. Lou carried a small black bag. He knocked, and the door was opened a few inches by Elwell. Redding crashed into it. The door swung wide. He hooked Elwell in the stomach with a left of false force. Elwell, a perfect actor, fell to the floor, gasping.

"Reach!" Lou called. His voice was crisp and authoritative.

Six men, five in shirtsleeves, one in a coat and tie (that was Nick), sat around a money-strewn table. Nick had been dealing. Very slowly, holding the deck, he raised his hands into the air.

There was a sharp explosion. Smoke curled from Stahal's gun. A youngish man slumped forward, his head hitting the table. Then he half-raised himself. The front of his white shirt was bloodstained.

Outside in the corridor Herbert Wilson hurriedly slipped into a face mask and, deserting his lookout post, rushed into the room. Stahal said, "I couldn't help it. The guy didn't raise his hands fast enough."

Herbert Wilson assumed charge. "Go over to the wall," he ordered the players who were holding their hands aloft. "Face it and keep your hands up. Nobody better move."

Everyone but the wounded man, a former professional baseball player named Lou Garrett, and Nick obeyed with alacrity. Nick put his arm around Garrett, who did not seem too badly hurt, and helped him to the wall. Showing no fear, Nick addressed Herbert Wilson: "This man needs medical attention."

Wilson made no reply.

"Robbery is one thing," Nick told him, "but murder is another. You can get away with the first, not the second."

Pulling a handkerchief from his pocket, Wilson handed it to Nick. "See what you can do to help him."

Nick attempted to stem the flow of blood.

Wilson scooped up the money, stuffing it into the bag his brother carried. He nodded toward Redding, who went to the telephone wires and jerked them from the wall. Then the four men began backing out of the suite.

Elwell was still on the floor. He was groaning.

Last to leave was Herbert Wilson, who flung the warning:

"No one better leave this room for ten minutes if they don't want their head blown off."

The door banged shut.

The four men went downstairs by different routes, rendezvoused in Wilson's car, and drove away to park on a deserted road and count the money. They had completely forgotten to lift wallets and take rings from fingers. There was nearly $200,000 in the black satchel.

Wilson said emphatically, "No more heists of poker games." He turned toward Stahal. "And no more of you. We're through. You understand?"

Stahal said that he did. Two years later he was shot in Chicago by a mobster. Redding was killed at a railroad crossing the same year, as he was making a getaway from a bank job. Lou Wilson died in an exchange of gunfire with a Standard Oil Company office watchman in Toledo. Herbert Wilson, the mastermind of the mob, spent twelve years in San Quentin and six years in Kingston Penitentiary, Canada.

None of the heisted men took Garrett to the hospital, where it would have been necessary to fill out a police report. One of them knew a doctor who wouldn't ask questions. He patched up Garrett. It turned out to be only a flesh wound.

Out of the nearly $200,000 swept from the table, only about $5,000 belonged to Nick. His pocket contained over $120,000. He didn't seem to mind what had transpired. To a friend he remarked, "It was a night of action and that's what I was looking for."

When Herbert Wilson was seventy-eight years old, he wrote a letter of apology to Nick, fully explaining the evening of the heist at the Alexandria Hotel, and inviting him to come up to Canada where he was living, for some fishing. He concluded with: "We really ought to get together—the King of the Gamblers and the King of the Safecrackers."

For one of the few times in his life, with the exception of correspondence with his sister Maria in Athens, Nick wrote a letter. He thanked Wilson for his truthfulness and said that he bore him no grudge. He mentioned that what happened long ago was just "footprints on the sands of time." The fishing invitation was politely declined. Regarding it, he said, "It is a little too slow for me, but I understand that fish are becoming smarter every year, and when they learn to play poker that is when I'll come up to British Columbia and visit you."

Only once—back in Chicago on November 21, 1920—did Nick's name appear on a police blotter. On that date he was caught in a raid when the bunco squad crashed a basement crap game. Along with a dozen or so of the participants he was taken into custody.

The judge, after hearing the facts, set the bail at $500.

"This is a tempest in a teapot," Nick said to His Honor. Reaching under his coat he opened a money belt, brought out a number of thousand dollar bills, and stood bail for the lot.

Reporters swarmed around him, firing questions, which he steadfastly refused to answer. Finally he bowed to the most persistent one: "Count the money in your belt."

Nick obliged. The total was $398,000. The newspapers had a field day. It made one of those stories the public loves to read—how a vagrant was carrying around a small fortune in cash.

When a bailbondsman told Nick that he hoped for the Greek's sake that none of his friends skipped town and left him holding the bag, Nick replied sorrowfully, "Yes, it would be a tragedy to me."

Startled, the bailbondsman said, "I didn't think money meant *that* much to you."

"Oh, it wouldn't be the loss of money," Nick answered to set him straight. "If they blew the town I might have a hard time finding another game as good as this one."

After exhausting most of the action in and around Los Angeles, Nick headed for Louisville and the Kentucky Derby. At the Derby he was a heavy loser, but more than made up for his losses in several poker games. Next stop was Hot Springs, Arkansas. He boarded the train with a tout named Herman, who had always been lucky for him. Just the sight of him at any track, in his loud clothes, talking in a confidential tone out of the side of his mouth to anyone who would listen, amused Nick and kept him in a good humor throughout the day.

In the huge Derby crowd Nick hadn't seen Herman. Afterward he saw him in a hotel lobby. Herman had gone broke, and Nick staked him to a ticket to Hot Springs. They boarded the train together. It was noon. Nick invited the tout to have lunch with him. The offer was readily accepted.

They made their way to the dining car. Once seated, Nick opened a Louisville newspaper to start reading an article on Albert Einstein and his contributions to theoretical physics and his work on the photoelectric effect. He found it fascinating reading, and when the waiter came around he was hardly conscious of his presence.

The waiter placed the customary pad used on trains for the diners to write out their own orders. Nick paid no attention, but kept on reading how Einstein had developed the quantum theory of specific heat.

Herman broke into his concentration by asking, "Nick, what do you want to eat?"

Nick didn't wish to be disturbed. "Oh, anything," he mumbled.

"Anything?"

Nick lowered his newspaper. "Anything you order for yourself, Herman, order for me."

"Goddam it!" Herman's voice rose, "tell me what you want."

"Listen, Herman," said Nick, dropping the newspaper in front of him on the table. "It's very simple. Just order me anything you want to—anything from a brontosaurus steak to an ostrich egg."

"Huh?" Herman's jaw dropped.

"Please," Nick said, "anything. I don't care what it is."

He picked up the newspaper again, and Herman told the waiter what he wanted, requesting the same for Nick.

The waiter left for the kitchen. Nick continued reading. Finishing, he folded the paper neatly and placed it in a vacant chair next to him just as the waiter set three dishes in front of him: mashed potatoes, boiled potatoes, lyonnaise potatoes, and a cup of coffee. Nick glanced in front of Herman and saw the same order.

He stared at the tout.

Herman hung his head sheepishly, then explained, "I just had a yen for potatoes, Nick, that's all."

"Too many carbohydrates," Nick told him.

"Huh?" Herman was puzzled.

After explaining the starch content of potatoes, Nick called the waiter back and wrote down a complete luncheon for both himself and Herman. He picked up the newspaper and handed it upside down to Herman.

"Interesting article on Einstein," Nick said. "Thought you might like to read it."

Herman took the newspaper in the same upside-down position and buried his nose in it, thus confirming Nick's suspicions. The man couldn't read or write.

Retelling the story at Hot Springs, he concluded with, "He had the necessary educational qualities for a good tout."

Hot Springs, located southwest of Little Rock in the Ouachita Mountains, was a wide-open town throughout the 1920s. A man could gamble all night and, to recuperate, could drop into one of the forty-seven hot springs within a short taxi ride of any hotel. Nick was a believer in the therapeutic value of steam baths, steam cabinets, and hot mineral water. Evaluating these treatments, he said, "Maybe they won't actually cure anything, but they can prepare a sinner for Hades so that he can know in advance what temperatures to expect."

If Nick harbored any thought that he was the sole possessor

of the title of Nick the Greek, he learned differently his first day in Hot Springs. At lunch he was introduced to Nick the Greek Spiros from New Orleans. That same evening he crossed paths with Nick the Greek Romanidou from Philadelphia, Nick the Greek Poulaki from Denver, and Nick the Greek Papadopoulos from Miami.

"All pretenders to your throne and would-be usurpers," a friend said, predicting, "the dice and the cards will determine who the real Nick the Greek is."

His third night in Hot Springs found Nick the focal point in a memorable game. Those who recall this game, and whose memories are undimmed by the passing of the years, credit Nick for one of his greatest exhibitions of coolness, efficiency, skill, and verve. He was one of the players in a seven-handed stud poker game staged in a hotel room. The game had an inflexible rule: it was freeze-out, and anyone who lost $20,000 had to drop out.

Word of the game had been whispered about, and the room was crowded with kibitzers. Nick didn't particularly relish kibitzers, but it was a way of life accepted by the gamblers. He once compared them to "educated remora, or sucking fish" (the fish that cling to the underbelly of a shark and share in his food).

At the end of the second day only two players remained, Nick and a lawyer of questionable reputation from St. Louis. The remainder had lost their initial investment and been eliminated. The lawyer, an arrogant man, was what gamblers call a "poor winner." He sneered, emoted, and swore like a trooper.

But he was winning.

"I don't suppose," he said to Nick, "you'd be willing to wager a hundred thousand dollars on the final outcome?" His tone was patronizing.

"Your supposition is incorrect," Nick answered. "The bet is on."

Nick's bankroll began slipping. The timing was perfect for

the kibitzers to jump into the act and offer Nick side bets. He took them all, for a total of $75,000.

He continued to lose. Twice he was barely high-carded. His bankroll nose-dived to less than $3,000. The lawyer was ready for the final blow. His face held a smirk as he raked in a small pot. "I'll have your ass in a few more hands," he boasted, "and another goddamned Greek will go down the drain."

Nick held his tongue.

"I hope you can borrow enough to pay off these bastardly kibitzers," he taunted.

Nick lit one of his long cigars and blew a thick smoke ring. After watching it break up in the air, he said to his opponent, "There's only one thing I'm going to have to borrow, Mr. Lawyer."

"What's that?" the lawyer asked.

"A larger vocabulary for you so that you can eliminate some of the profanity."

The lawyer scowled and picked up the cards, shuffling noisily. In a flash the complexion of the game changed. Lady Luck took a seat on Nick's lap. He could do nothing wrong. Within the next three hours he won forty-five of fifty hands.

The game ended.

Nick stood up, said to the lawyer, "Goodnight," and started from the room.

"Hey, Greek!" the lawyer called after him.

Nick stopped in his tracks.

"Do you always run away as soon as you win a score?"

The room grew deathly quiet. No one moved. Nick wheeled, headed for the table, his eyes fastened on the lawyer, who half rose from his chair, not knowing what to expect. Nick picked up the blue-backed deck of cards, riffled the pack eight times, cut twice, and spread them face down in front of the lawyer.

"Pull one," he said. "High card wins five hundred thousand."

Slowly the lawyer settled into his seat. The only sound in

the room was breathing. The seconds ticked by, running into minutes. Once the lawyer's right hand made a spasmodic movement toward the spread-out cards, only to retreat in slow motion. His face, drained of color, was ghost-white. His entire body seemed frozen stiff, his eyes abnormally dilated, staring agonizingly at the cards.

When it became obvious that the lawyer was in some form of trauma, Nick walked away from the table, through the ranks of kibitzers who parted for him, and out the door.

One of the original players caught up to him on the street. "You're the King, Nick," he praised.

Nick shook his head. "No," he disputed, "Arnold Rothstein's the King."

"You can take him, Nick."

Nick paused and said evenly, "That's what I'm going to find out within a few days."

A Visit to the Promised Land

THE year was 1925, and along the Great White Way in New York there was an air of expectancy among the sporting gentry. Daily they asked an unanswered question:

When is he coming to town?

Reference was to Nick the Greek. The bonanzas he had struck in San Francisco, Chicago, Los Angeles, and Hot Springs were the talk of the town. Any doubts or uncertainties that he wouldn't arrive were banished by clear-thinking members of the gambling fraternity. It was only a matter of when. They knew of the compulsion, the lure, the magnet, the tentacles of temptation that would eventually draw the gentlemanly Greek to the Promised Land.

The gambling climate was different here in New York. The stakes were higher, the expertise widespread. The mark, the tinhorn, the sucker, were easily devoured by the Eastern clique. To them, any cities west of Weehawken were cowtowns peopled by undesigning idiots.

Kingpin of them all was Arnold Rothstein. Members of his high-flying echelon included Joe Starr, the Wall Street broker; Leo Kaplis, gentleman gambler from New Jersey; Sam

Rosoff, loud and boisterous subway contractor and a Tammany behind-the-scenes manipulator; George McManus, bookmaker extraordinaire; Jimmy Meehan, florid-faced gambler and grifter; Alvin C. (Titanic) Thompson, a willing bettor on any sport; Meyer and brother Sam Boston, gamblers and stock market plungers; Martin Bowe, bookmaker; Joe Bernstein and Big Bill Dwyer, gamblers.

This was the reception committee waiting to welcome Nick as his train chugged into Pennsylvania Station. They were restless. St. Patrick's Day had just passed, with loads of devotion shown for the wearin' o' the green. The delegation at the railroad station was also devoted to the color green. But this particular green stood for money—fresh, crisp, and crackly—that they hoped the Greek would bring in abundance with him. And depart without.

Armed with no advance description of his noted fraternity brother, each carried a different mental picture of the man born in Crete. The individual guesses as to his appearance blended into a composite of a wide-lapeled, pin-striped suit cut to accommodate shoulder holsters; a heavy, square-jawed face; large and hairy hands; and a raucous voice.

They couldn't believe their eyes!

Before them stood a strikingly handsome and dashing figure of a man, graceful and cultivated, whose voice was soft and manner professorial. In one hand he held a book, and in the other a small, brown satchel. He was following a redcap carrying his large suitcase.

Jimmy Meehan shook his head. "He ain't one of us," he whispered.

He certainly wasn't.

As the tall figure of the Greek came into view, one of the group, after inspecting him from head to toe, remarked, "Doesn't look like he has a dime."

"But," argued another, "his clothes are smart."

"Anyone can get those," came the answer, and it was

pointed out, "the luggage is what counts. A dead giveaway. Look at that old, cracked, worn satchel he's carrying."

The satchel he indicated contained $1,400,000.

Arnold Rothstein detached himself from the group and approached Nick.

"I'm Rothstein," he said, offering his hand. It was a soft hand, almost like baby flesh. To Nick a soft hand usually meant a hard head.

"I'm Dandolos," he said.

Rothstein said, "Welcome to New York."

Nick rode away with Rothstein in a chauffeur-driven Rolls Royce. Rothstein, whose sharp eyes seldom missed anything, was quick to note the lack of luggage.

"You're traveling rather light, Nick," he observed.

"The vagabond, when rich, is called a tourist, and I'd dislike being called one," Nick answered.

Rothstein made no comment. He leaned forward and called to the chauffeur, "Alamic Hotel, George."

Side by side, blanketed in silence, rode the two foremost gamblers in America. Each was thinking about the other.

Rothstein was sitting on a mythical throne, well entrenched. No one had been able to knock him from his exalted position. He was known as The Brain, the sponsor of "floating" crap games, which he had started in about 1912.

He had two favorite expressions. Most commonly used was "I'm a hundred percent right." The other was an ominous one, uttered when someone threatened not to pay a debt owed him: "God help you, if you don't."

He was a man of small stature, barely exceeding five feet, seven inches. His face was colorless, inexpressive, immobile. His eyes didn't seem to belong. To many they were constantly laughing. But actually, they masked his true inner feelings. They were restlessly roving, like a detective seeking to uncover or detect some pertinent evidence.

Once Rothstein played against a small-time gambler who

was confident of holding his own in a high stakes game. This man, a student of physiognomy, took one searching look at Rothstein's face and believed (or so he told a friend) that he had discovered his temperament, character, and mannerisms.

"It'll be easy to get a tell on him," he boasted.

To his surprise and consternation, the face that resembled an open book before the start of the game snapped shut the moment the cards were dealt. The small-time gambler had his brains beaten out.

Rothstein had a variety of interests. Once he owned the Brook, one of Saratoga's most fashionable gambling casinos, and a stable of horses—one of which, Sporting Blood, pulled off perhaps the richest coup in the history of turfdom when he beat Harry Payne Whitney's Prudery and Rothstein pocketed $450,000. He held real estate, securities, and large bank accounts, besides being a silent partner in many gambling and theatrical enterprises, including the backing of the record-breaking play *Abie's Irish Rose*. Sports celebrities, political bosses, social registrants, business tycoons, stage and movie stars were his confidants, often asking his advice.

Like Nick, Rothstein dressed in the manner of Park Avenue rather than that of Broadway, but the similarity ended there. They were poles apart in thought and deed, and a code of honesty, which Rothstein could dispense with if necessary.

Later, after a study of his adversary, Nick said to Rothstein, "Arnold, the basic difference in our gambling is very apparent. You gamble for greed. I gamble for thrills."

After mulling this over, Rothstein replied, "But you can't eat thrills."

"True," Nick said, "but neither can you replace them by anything."

Before they reached the hotel, Rothstein suggested, "Perhaps after you get settled you'd like to try your luck?"

Nick smiled and, pointing at his luggage, said, "It won't take me long to unpack."

Installed at the Alamac, Nick had hardly finished a shower when the telephone rang. It was Rothstein. Did Nick care to roll the dice a little that evening? That would be just fine, Nick told him. Rothstein furnished directions for finding the game.

He was to go to a certain midtown Manhattan hotel near midnight. A man would be sitting in a chair near the elevator. Nick was to nod to him. The man, in turn, would nod to the Negro elevator boy, who would whisk Nick up to the floor where the game was being held.

The staging of a floating crap game had to be meticulously planned. Should gunmen get wind of the location they had easy pickings. No one would go to the police even if he recognized the stickup men. It was part of the code of the underworld, a code that was as important to these men of questionable honor as the Constitution of the United States is to most citizens. Even if you were shot and knew you were dying, and the police sergeant was bent over you, pleading, "Tell me who did it, Joe," you were honor-bound not to disclose the identity of the rod man.

After a doorman had frisked him carefully, Nick, money satchel in hand, entered a good-sized room. A crowd of four deep surrounded a pool table. He could see only the backs of heads, but he heard someone who was managing the game call, "Ten's the point! Get your bets down!"

"Forty thousand to twenty . . . no, ten!" Nick called loudly.

"Bet," he heard someone say.

He worked his way toward the table, and as he did so he made additional bets, taking the customary 2–1 odds. It was impossible to see the dice over the heads of the players, but by the time he reached the table he heard the cry, "Ten the winner! The hard way! Coming out, next point!"

Nick had dropped an even $100,000 before he had his first glimpse of the layout!

Once he reached the table, he was given a royal welcome. He responded by taking all bets, as was his custom, against the dice. After the dice had worked their way halfway around the table, he came to the conclusion that—as he had suspected even before he started play—the players were all gunning for him. Everyone was shooting for his bankroll.

For him this was the zenith; he had transcended the heights of ecstasy and had climbed to the summit of enjoyment: Nick, alone, against everybody else. Who could ask for anything more delightful!

For eleven days the action continued unabated. Five times there were changes of location, the game moving from lofts to basements to avoid any heists. Periodically, members of New York's Finest—some still in uniform—dropped in to watch the action. None dared raid the game. Too many political powers were giving it the green light.

As the days flitted by until they seemed to merge into one, there were some notable highlights. At one point a shooter whose name Nick did not recall had nine as a point. Nick bet $200,000 against $300,000 that there would be no nine. The shooter promptly obliged him by throwing a seven on the next roll.

Nick was standing alongside Sam Rosoff. The heavy man, who had never heard of the word "diet," was perspiring freely; and so were the dice he was rolling, for they were red hot. Rosoff's point was eight, and Nick, glancing at the pile of bills in front of the subway contractor (a few hundreds were showing atop the stack), said he would bet it at odds of 6–5.

"You're on," Rosoff said.

He threw a five, a four—and up came eight.

"How much do I owe you, Sam?" Nick inquired.

Rosoff picked up the bills. "Well, let's see now," he said casually, beginning to count. He peeled off three hundred-dollar bills from the top, to expose seventy-nine thousand-dollar bills underneath.

From then on Nick began to slide downhill. Some of the money went to Rothstein, but most of it was divided around the table. Near midnight of the eleventh day Nick faded nine gentlemen a total of $110,000. Rothstein was throwing the dice.

The point was six. Wearily, Nick hunched over the table and saw the dice come up six.

"Gentlemen," he announced, "that does it for me. It's been a real pleasure." Opening the brown satchel, he paid off the bet. The satchel was empty. He had a ten-dollar bill in his pocket, all he had in the world. Starting for the door, he felt a tap on his shoulder. It was George McManus, who suggested they get something to eat.

"On one condition," Nick stipulated.

McManus asked what it was.

"That I pick up the check," Nick said.

McManus stared hard at him, as if not believing what he heard. He knew of the vast sum Nick had lost; he himself had come out $150,000 ahead.

"As you wish, Nick," he agreed.

Over scrambled eggs Nick mentioned that he was leaving town in a day or two, but that he would return in the near future and would like to try his luck again.

"Against Arnold?" McManus asked.

"Yes, of course against Arnold."

"Dice or poker?"

"Poker the next time."

McManus said, "It can be arranged."

Nick spent the next morning on the telephone making long-distance calls. Tapped out, he needed money. It was comparatively easy to raise. His credit rating was in a class by itself. He had never failed to meet a marker. Many felt honored to make him a loan.

Lunching at Lindy's, he traded stories with friends and acquaintances. Walter Winchell, sitting in, asked permission to print some that Nick had told. Nick politely refused, claiming it might offend or hurt a few people.

Just then he reached for a handkerchief. A dime came out with it, rolling onto the floor. He got down under the table and recovered it.

"That's one story I'm going to print," Winchell said, and the next day it appeared in his nationally syndicated column.

Big Bill Dwyer approached him. After shaking his head, Bill remarked, "Nick, I don't know how you do it. You lose a fortune, show no nerves, and keep smiling. Are you really upset and crying inside?"

"Not at all," Nick told him. "The greatest pleasure in my lige is gambling and winning. The next greatest pleasure is gambling and losing. So how can I be nervous or sad?"

As Nick was about to enter his hotel that evening, a uniformed chauffeur stepped in front of him. "Mr. Dandolos?"

Nick waited.

"I have something for you."

He handed Nick an unsealed envelope. Inside was a note from Arnold Rothstein. He read: "Please accept the car, the chauffeur, and what's in the rear seat, as a gift from me to a great loser."

Touching Nick's elbow, the chauffeur pointed, "Here it is, sir."

Nick, following his finger, saw a shiny new Rolls Royce parked at the curb. Someone indistinguishable was seated in the back seat. He walked over to the car and opened the door.

"Good evening, Mr. Dandolos," a woman's voice greeted.

Inside, expensively gowned, sat a raven-haired beauty. She smiled, flashing a row of dazzling white teeth. Nick recognized the fragrance of Christmas Night in the air. He didn't know quite what to say.

"I am rendered temporarily speechless," he managed.

The girl wasn't. She said, "Whatever prosperous hour Providence bestows upon you, receive it with a thankful hand: and defer not the enjoyment of the comforts of life."

"Good God!" Nick exclaimed, flabbergasted. "That's from Horace."

The girl said that he was right.

He kept inspecting her, pleased at what he saw. "Someone —and I don't think we have to mention his name—has coached you well," he complimented, and asked, "Do you know any more quotations?"

The girl gave a tinkling laugh. "No," she admitted, "but I hope that the one I just recited has a clear meaning?"

Nick reached out his hand and helped the girl from the car. "The meaning is perfectly clear," he said.

After making garaging arrangements for the car, he dismissed the chauffeur for the night. As for the girl, he took her arm, escorted her through the hotel lobby, into the elevator, and up to his room. His intentions were both educational and physical. He would supplement her knowledge of the ancient philosopher Horace—and acquaint her with a modern Greek philosopher named Nicholas Andrea Dandolos.

Operation Bounceback

GIRDED for action and heavily in debt, Nick hopped a train for Los Angeles. The Southern California city had generally been a lucky one for him, and here, starting from scratch, he hoped to rebuild his shrunken fortunes.

No one was at the station to see him off.

Taunts of the New York mob were still ringing in his ears. Someone had dubbed him "Saint Nick," and making the rounds was the somewhat humiliating jingle "Have no fear, Nick the Greek has left here."

His financial difficulties were soon overcome. He became involved in a game of lowball poker, starting with a borrowed $8,000. He had gone to the game with a close friend and admirer, Joe Benjamin, the skillful boxer. At the end of the fourth day of continuous play Nick had run his original investment up to $75,000.

Benjamin begged him to quit.

Nick paid no heed to his advice. The other players would go home for a spell, sleep, and return refreshed. Nick never left. Benjamin, who felt protective toward Nick (when it probably should have been the other way around), believed that the Greek, by holding his post, was jeopardizing his winnings. To Benjamin, seeing the other players return rested and eager was like seeing fresh troops attack a besieged garrison.

In order to make Nick quit, Benjamin knew he must do a little scheming—devise some clever ruse that Nick couldn't see through. He sought out Jack Dempsey, also a good pal of Nick's, and explained the situation.

"What do you want me to do?" Jack asked, eager to assist. "Go in and knock everyone out but Nick?"

Benjamin's plan called for nothing so drastic. Dempsey agreed to lend his support. He accompanied Benjamin to the game, watched for a few minutes, then nudged Nick.

"Nick," he said, "you've got to help me."

Excusing himself, Nick left the table and walked to a corner of the room with the champion to hear his problem.

"My combinations seem off," Dempsey began, "too sluggish. Maybe it's my timing. I wish you'd come over to my training quarters and see if you can straighten things out. That is," he added, "if you're not too tired."

"Tired!" Nick echoed, as if he had never heard of the word. "Of course not. Let's go."

Nick had always considered himself an astute sports authority, particularly on boxing. When he left with Dempsey and Benjamin, he was a $70,000 winner. Dempsey slipped into his trunks, punched the bag a few times, and Nick rained instructions upon him.

After Joe Benjamin had been beaten by Ace Hudkins, the Nebraska Wildcat, he was finished in the ring, and Nick—despite his previous adventures with an unwanted bodyguard—took on Benjamin in the role. He was the last man to need protection, but he was fond of Benjamin as a companion; thus the working arrangement.

Meanwhile, Hudkins secured a bout with Ruby Goldstein, idol of the Eastern fight fans. Goldstein, an undefeated lightweight contender, was the perfect picture boxer, possessing every attribute necessary to elevate him to the top. His chief assets were the heart of a lion, dazzling footwork, speed, and a knockout punch in either hand.

Gamblers had him a 6–1 favorite over Hudkins.

Reasoned Nick to Benjamin, "Anyone who can beat you is my betting choice."

"Not necessarily," Benjamin countered. "Something I ate the night of the fight might have thrown me off."

"Fighters are alibi artists," Nick stated, and reminded Benjamin, "you were lucky to be able to eat for a week after the fight."

Taking the odds, Nick laid $90,000 on the Nebraskan.

From the first round it appeared to be a one-sided contest. Goldstein, exhibiting the footwork of a ballet dancer, whirled around the clumsy Hudkins, jabbing him at will, running up a tremendous point lead.

Undiscouraged, Nick kept taking bets from ringsiders. With the passing of each round the odds lengthened, until he was getting as high as 10–1 on some of his healthy wagers.

In the middle of the sixth round Goldstein got in a sneak punch that sent Hudkins sprawling on his back in the center of the canvas. No sooner had the underdog hit the deck than he bounced to his feet and tore into a bewildered Goldstein. His flailing fists became windmills of destruction, and it was quite apparent why he had been cognomenized Wildcat.

Before the round ended, it was Goldstein who was stretched on the ring floor, counted out.

There was a certain similarity between Nick's killing on the Goldstein–Hudkins fight and his wagering tactics on the Alabama–Washington Rose Bowl Game in 1926—the difference being that Nick knew little about football and much about boxing.

Football talk was filling the air with the approach of New Year, and fans were awaiting the titanic battle between the Southern and the West Coast representatives. Nick heard it wherever he went. It became infectious. Soon he began to acquire a football vocabulary. Actually, all he knew about the sport was that twenty-two young men were fighting for possession of an inflated rubber bladder wrapped in the skin of a pig.

At least, however, he was more knowledgeable about the game than a young lady whom he sporadically dated. As he spoke of the upcoming gridiron battle, the lady admitted not being conversant with football, and asked, "How many quarters are there?"

They were dining and it was dessert time. A bowl of fruit graced the table. Among the assortment was an apple. Nick reached for it, picked up a knife and cut the piece of fruit into four pieces.

"How many quarters are there to this apple?" he questioned.

"Four," she estimated brightly.

"Right," Nick agreed, adding, "and that's how many quarters to a football game."

The lady smiled. "I'm learning rapidly."

"Yes, my dear," Nick responded, trying to keep a straight face.

As the day of the game approached, Nick read everything he could concerning it. One sportswriter would favor Washington, the next Alabama. He was in a quandary, so he consulted his friend Mark Hellinger.

"Bet Alabama," the New York newspaperman advised.

Calling several reliable bookmakers, Nick got down on the team from below the Mason-Dixon Line. Hellinger's advice was good enough for him. He was an admirer of the Eastern writer and read everything he wrote. For some reason or other, the two failed ever to have dinner together. A wag stated what might have happened if such had occurred:

"Smart managers would have sent their fighters around to study the speed of their rights and lefts," he said. "They were the two fastest check grabbers in America."

Nick attended the gridiron classic and watched Washington roll up a modest lead in the first half. Alabama couldn't seem to get untracked. Every long drive ended with a fumble. Nick climbed to the press box to confer with Hellinger.

"Don't give it a thought, Nick," Hellinger said lightly. "There's a lot of football left. Alabama will come on strong."

Hellinger was convincing. Nick made additional bets on the Crimson Tide at long odds. Lighting a cigar, he sat back in his seat, waiting. He didn't have to wait long. It was a fired-up Alabama team, one that could do nothing wrong, led by Johnny Mack Brown, handsome backfield star who was later to become a motion picture actor.

Alabama eked out a 20–19 victory. Nick was $46,000 richer than when he had gone through the turnstiles to take a seat.

Hellinger was a great kidder. "You see?" he said to Nick. "The outcome was never in doubt."

While Nick may have been a neophyte at football, baseball was more to his understanding. Here his memory served him well. He was a sitting encyclopedia. He had made an extensive study of the diamond sport with much the same thoroughness that he employed on horse racing, poker, and dice. He kept individual charts on the batters, probably just as accurate as those big-league statisticians keep today. He knew the batting averages, pitching abilities, and idiosyncrasies of most of the regular players in the Pacific Coast League. He would attend games with friends, and the side bets would fly thick and fast. One of the group was Walter McGinley, a successful oil prospector, overlooked in most gambling histories, but one of the biggest baseball bettors who ever lived.

Nick and McGinley bet nearly every pitch—whether it would be a ball or a strike and what the batter might do. One afternoon when the Los Angeles Angels were engaging the San Francisco Seals at Wrigley Field, Nick propositioned, "I'll take a thousand dollars to fifty that the next batter is hit by a pitched ball."

The bet was immediately covered.

The batter, with the count three and two, was hit on the leg, and as he limped toward first base, Nick, collecting $1,000, jokingly remarked, "I had inside information."

"Come on, quit kidding," a friend entreated. "Wasn't it a hunch bet?"

"Of course not," Nick denied. "I only bet on percentages. Scientifically. The batter had a larger stomach than his teammates and it's an inch and a half closer to the plate."

There were no more questions.

Discoursing on baseball gambling, Nick said, "It's a wonderful action game, with something going on every few minutes. For the gamblers the only improvement would be for the pitchers to pitch faster."

Nick was of the opinion that no two gamblers were alike. "It may, to the untutored, seem so," he said, "but each is an individual in his manner of playing. The only similarity between them is that sometimes they win, sometimes they lose."

One of the few he socialized with for any length of time was Alvin C. (Titanic) Thompson. Thompson enjoyed a national reputation that rose rapidly to the legend class. He wasn't strictly a gambler, but a man who would pull a cute caper if given the opportunity. He willingly bet on anything, trivial or important—mostly freak wagers taken by suckers who, in turn, were taken themselves. A calm, patient man, Thompson had iron nerves. There wasn't a card game invented that he wouldn't play. And he was considered a firearms authority and crack shot with rifle, shotgun, or pistol.

Perhaps his outstanding achievement was as a golfer. Just how good he was, no one ever knew. He might win by a single stroke over a twenty-handicap player and do an encore the next day against a two-handicap shooter. The higher the stakes, the steadier his game. It was said of his golf game that if he were playing on a course laid out in a demilitarized zone with warring troops flanking it and firing at each other across the no-man's-land area, the effect on Titanic's eighteen-hole total would be negligible.

His chief pleasure in life was to trap a victim in a trumped-up caper—not so much for the financial gain but for the feeling of conquest. Even Nick was taken by the improvisations of the Oklahoma-born con artist.

The first such occurrence happened in New York. On a gusty day when Nick and Titanic were walking down Broadway, they passed a peanut stand. Titanic halted before it, pointed to the top of a seven-story building.

"Wind and all," he said, "I'll bet I can throw a peanut to the roof."

Nick glanced at the peanut stand and the seven-story building, making some rapid calculations.

"It's a bet."

They agreed on an amount.

Titanic bought a bag of peanuts and, extending them toward Nick, said, "Pick one for me."

Reaching in, Nick selected one of average size and dropped it into Titanic's hand. Winding up first like a baseball pitcher on the mound, he threw the peanut straight up to the roof of the building. Without comment Nick handed him $500. Then he reached into the bag, took a handful of peanuts, and began munching them.

"You told me once you didn't like peanuts," Titanic said.

"I didn't when they cost only a dime," Nick said.

After making a few inquiries, Nick learned that this wasn't the first time that Titanic had pulled the peanut trick, and he learned of its artful design. In his pocket Titanic carried a special doctored peanut, which had been opened carefully, stuffed with lead, and glued together again. For a sleight-of-hand master such as Titanic, it was easy to palm the peanut selected from the bag and then throw the special one.

"I didn't mind being slickered," Nick said, "because the odds were right."

In the 1920s there was no horse racing around Los Angeles except at fairgrounds. To see them run meant crossing the Mexican border into Tijuana and proceeding a few miles to the track at Agua Caliente. Accommodations being superior in San Diego, Nick and Thompson stayed at the U. S. Grant Hotel in that city for a week and drove to the track daily in Titanic's car.

The distance was exactly eleven miles to the border.

After the conclusion of the races, as they were clearing the Customs preparatory to heading northward to San Diego, Titanic casually mentioned, "I ought to be able to reach the San Diego city limits in five minutes."

Nick did some figuring. The traffic was heavy. It was a two-lane road. Titanic would have to drive at a rate exceeding 120 miles per hour to make good his boast.

"Impossible," Nick stated.

"Five thousand says I can," Thompson offered.

"You're on," Nick returned. He set the dashboard clock at five minutes before the hour of six.

"Go!" he encouraged, and warned, "Try to see that one of us remains alive to collect the bet."

In exactly four and one-half minutes of modest driving a sign hove into view: SAN DIEGO—CITY LIMITS.

"I can't believe it," Nick said, plainly puzzled.

Titanic said, "Seeing is believing."

Nick reached into his wallet, handed Titanic five thousand-dollar bills. "The city just couldn't have grown that fast in one afternoon," he complained.

Subsequently he made the discovery that Titanic, with the help of a confederate, had uprooted the sign in the early hours of the morning to transplant it farther down the highway.

Some years later when Nick was reminded of this chicanery, he said that Titanic's tricks paled into nothingness compared with some of the didoes of the infamous "Yellow Kid" Weil, a noted midwestern confidence man. By luck Nick barely escaped one of Weil's traps.

They were riding a train together from St. Louis to Chicago, and Nick suggested a game of pinochle or some type of rummy to while away the hours. Weil was far too shrewd to buck heads with Nick, and he said so. Try as they might, they couldn't come up with a game that provided them with an equal chance at winning. They went into the dining car for lunch, and Weil ordered an extra pat of butter for his sandwich. As they finished the train stopped, and Weil, excusing himself, said he was going to stretch his legs a little at the station.

Nick glanced out the window and saw it was raining hard. Strange time, he thought, for a man to exercise. Also that extra pat of butter. He hadn't seen Weil use it on his sandwich, but it was gone. There was something odd going on. Walking to the end of the car, Nick put his head out and spotted Weil, who didn't see him. The con man was spreading butter on the window of Nick's compartment.

Back in the compartment Weil made a suggestion: They should take raindrops on opposite sides of the window, and the first ones to reach bottom would make the winner.

"Just for few hundred to make it interesting," Weil proposed.

Nick examined the rain hitting the windowpane and forming into drops. The drops on his side stopped and started and took winding routes. On Weil's side he noticed that they fell swift and straight.

The butter had greased the glass on Nick's side.

Nick offered, "I'll play only if you change seats with me."

Weil, of course, didn't agree to that and said, "Maybe we better think of something else."

Instead they talked—and had little in common.

* * *

When Nick's rapidly expanding bankroll reached the million dollar mark, he returned to New York—objective: Arnold Rothstein. This time the battlefield would be a poker table. Rothstein had always said, "The man with the most money at the start of the game will be the winner." Nick didn't entirely agree with this pronouncement and meant to prove his point.

But before the showdown with Rothstein he wanted to have some fun. Fun meant dinners, girls, shows. In this respect Nick helped the Roaring Twenties to roar louder. He knew the entire chorus line in the Ziegfeld Follies and dated most of them. He treated the girls like queens—they never lacked food, flowers, and costly gifts while Nick was on the scene. The astonishing thing to the chorus beauties was that the Greek demanded nothing in return for the favors he bestowed upon them. He threw restaurant parties lasting two to three days, with the tab running into thousands of dollars. Many of these hours were consumed by him on the dance floor; he was a truly accomplished dancer with a great sense of rhythm, whirling his partners gracefully in all the steps of the day.

Gradually Nick began shedding his bevy of beauties until only one remained: Florence O'Dennison, a featured dancer. Every night found him dressed in evening clothes, front row center, and he was with her from the moment she left her dressing room.

Some nights when he took Miss O'Dennison home early, he sought action in crap games with gamblers of a somewhat lesser standing in skill and money than those who took him to the cleaners on his initial visit to New York City.

One of these evenings found him in a rough basement dive on Third Avenue. Hoodlums, cutthroats, and just plain crooks thronged around a battered pool table. Overhead a strong shaded light illuminated a number of evil-favored faces.

Nick hung his overcoat on a rickety clothes rack, took up a

position at the table, played for an hour, didn't enjoy the game much, and decided to leave. He taxied to Lindy's, and no sooner had he sat down at a table with friends than he jumped up, complaining, "I'm certainly getting absentminded. I left my overcoat somewhere."

A voice piped up, "Proves nothing, Nick. It can happen to anyone."

"Not with sixty thousand dollars in one of his pockets," Nick told him.

The doorman whistled him down a cab, and he returned to the basement joint. He immediately sighted the overcoat, pulled it off the rack, and searched the right pocket. The money was still there, every cent of it.

Retelling the story the same night at Lindy's, he said, "The odds would be about thirty-five to one that both the coat and the money had gone south."

On other occasions through the years Nick had momentary lapses of memory, which luckily cost him nothing. In New York he sent $100,000 to the cleaners in the hip pocket of a pair of trousers and rushed out half an hour later to recover the money before the garment departed for the plant.

In Los Angeles he forgot $41,000 in the pocket of a sports jacket he left with a tailor for alterations. Again he recovered the money intact. Once he was in a car twenty miles from Victorville, California, a stop between Los Angeles and Las Vegas, when he suggested to the friend who was driving him, "Better go back to the restaurant, I left my hat on the rack."

"Forget it, Nick," his friend advised, pointing out, "What's a hat to you? It's a long way back. You can get another hat for ten bucks."

Nick said without emotion, "To replace this one, figuring ten for a new one, would cost eighty thousand and ten dollars."

His friend pulled over to the shoulder of the road and stopped the car, but before he could speak, Nick continued.

"Eight ten-thousand-dollar bills are hidden in the hatband."

Without a word his friend swung the car around, headed in the opposite direction. Back at the restaurant Nick found his hat hanging on the same hook as when he left, and what was more important, the money lay undisturbed behind the hatband.

Anyone for Poker?

NICK now felt he was again ready to tackle Rothstein and his hardcore associates. He let his intentions be known. Rothstein, the reigning King of Gamblers, was delighted. "My apartment," he said, setting a time and date.

The punctual Greek was the first to arrive at the New Yorker's sumptuous Manhattan quarters. Frequently chided for earliness, he had a favorite answer: "The only time lateness should be excused is at your own funeral."

Rothstein, like Nick, believed in punctuality. He once turned down a deal because a man was twenty minutes tardy for an appointment. It cost the latecomer a tidy sum. Rothstein himself would have turned a neat profit, but was more interested in teaching a lesson that might never be forgotten.

The game began. For the first hour Nick studied his opponents, focusing on their eyes, their hands, the muscles around their mouths, and the veins in their faces and necks; watching any mannerisms and excessive perspiring; and noticing how they breathed and swallowed and how fast or how slow they smoked.

With the beginning of the third hour his observations

started paying off. He began winning. By this time he knew his opponents well, with the exception of Arnold Rothstein. Rothstein's play was inconsistent, never falling into a pattern, and to read his face was hopeless. It had become a tightly frozen mask.

Nine hours ticked by. Nick was his usual fresh self. During the span of play he had eaten a small sandwich with the crusts cut off and had drunk the juice from two freshly squeezed oranges. After the first twenty-four hours he planned on a few sporadic sips of brandy.

By early morning he was ahead close to $700,000. Rothstein was also winning, but not as substantially. Then, without warning, the fickle Goddess of Luck did an about-face and everything Nick tried turned sour. The poker proverb "Chips have no home" was proving its validity as his stack vanished, to be replenished by more buying.

Rothstein was growing richer, the chips building up before him. Infrequently Nick gazed searchingly at him and Rothstein stared back. It was strictly between the two of them now. They were heading for a showdown. The other players had been hit staggering blows and lacked the chips in this high-table-stakes game to raise or call when they should, often having to settle for part of the pot.

Stud hands were dealt. Nick had a king in the hole and a king up. Rothstein had a queen of diamonds showing. The other players had low cards. Nick sat to the left of the dealer. It was his bet. Not wanting to drive anyone out, he bet a modest $10,000. Two players called, and it was up to Rothstein.

Rothstein raised the pot $30,000.

Nick called. The other players passed, leaving only Nick and Rothstein to fight it out. Nick guessed that Rothstein had an ace in the hole, but no matter what card it was—even another queen—*he* had a good thing going and meant to nurse it along.

His next card was an eight and Rothstein received a nine of diamonds. He had two diamonds showing, but there was no cause for alarm. Nick didn't give a possible flush a second thought. No player in his right mind, if he had three diamonds, would attempt to buck the percentages and try for two more. Not at the high stakes they were playing.

Nick bet another $10,000. Rothstein raised him $60,000. Nick just called.

For the next card Nick drew a five and Rothstein got a six of diamonds. Nick checked, and Rothstein counted out $90,000 in chips and calmly pushed them into the pot.

Nick picked up his half-smoked cigar from the ashtray and unhurriedly lit it. His concentration was on Rothstein's hands, which were resting on the table. They gave no clue. They were steady. Then Rothstein belched. It was a low belch, but to Nick, who hated unnecessary noise at a card game, it sounded like a cannon had been fired.

The odds seemed heavily stacked in his favor. He summarized the situation. Rothstein either had a pair of queens or an ace—possibly an ace of diamonds, which would give him four of the same suit. Yet even if he did have the four diamonds, the odds against him drawing the fifth were great.

The room was quiet. Everyone was watching Nick.

Nick called the $90,000, and raised the pot $188,500, every cent he had in front of him. Rothstein called. He still had chips left, but Nick was tapped out and the betting had ended.

There was $797,000 on the table, the biggest pot in the history of stud poker.

It was time for the final card. A seven of clubs fell to Nick, who stifled a yawn with the back of his hand. Rothstein was dealt a seven of diamonds.

Rothstein said, "Too bad you ran out of chips, Nick, or we could have made this an interesting pot."

Very slowly he turned his hole card over. It was an ace of diamonds, giving him a diamond flush.

Nick rose from the table. "Thank you, gentlemen," he said. "Once again it has been a pleasure."

Rothstein escorted him to the door. "You're a real sportsman," he complimented.

"Win without boasting. Lose without excuse," Nick said, quoting an American, Albert Payson Terhune.

That evening, acting as if he didn't have a care in the world, Nick dated Florence O'Dennison. She had never looked lovelier, and Nick had never been in a more mellow and romantic mood. He broached marriage, finding her willing. But with his bankroll badly mangled he didn't think the time propitious. He told her he was going back to Los Angeles for some business dealings and would send for her later.

"Any time," she told him. "I'll be waiting."

He left New York, a very unlucky city for him. Within the space of six weeks he had substantial sums of money in three safe deposit bank vaults and was well along on the road to recovery. Florence was constantly on his mind, and he long-distanced her nightly. Finally he told her he was ready and waiting for her. A date was set for her departure from New York.

Two months before he died, Nick recalled vividly the events that next transpired. He told me, "When a man has already crossed the threshold of his twilight years the present is a struggle, the future a question mark, the past a treasured memory to be relived again and again, with its joys and sorrows, ecstasy and pain.

"There is always one incident in the past that stands out with great clarity, and years later, in summing up, you ask yourself, Was it Circumstance, was it Fate, was it the Wheel of Fortune that dictated the turn of events?

"I like to believe it was the Goddess of Destiny holding me powerless in the palm of her hand, and mine was not to reason why, but helplessly to bow to her capricious whims."

He was referring to the outcome of a sequence of events

that was scheduled to start when he would step into the chauffeur-manned Rolls Royce he had had shipped from the East Coast and head for the Union Station to meet the transcontinental train from New York. Here he would stand at the end of the passenger ramp, holding a bouquet of American Beauty roses.

He would sight her from a distance, at first a blurred but beautiful vision, and then, gradually coming into sharp focus, the prettiest, the brightest, the most talented, and—beyond any doubt—the shapeliest dancer in the current edition of the Ziegfeld Follies.

Millionaires had offered the world on a platter to this girl. A foreign potentate had begged her to help him rule his kingdom. Members of New York's social Four Hundred and the Long Island horsey set had tendered her a life among the likes of the Vanderbilts, the Whitneys, and the Sloans.

Florence O'Dennison turned down all of them for Nicholas Andrea Dandolos—occupation: gambler.

Yes, Nick thought, she would be coming up that ramp, high heels clicking against the cement, and he would be waiting for her. He could almost hear her low, sultry voice, the tone of which vibrated his nerve ends. It was sort of a breathless purr, punctuated by tiny gasps.

And in that exciting voice, she would say, "How are you, Nick darling?"

And he would hear himself answer without emotion, "Fine, Flo."

There would be no embraces, no declarations of love. Not even a handshake. She knew he hated public demonstrations. Serious talking would come later.

Over a dish of spanakopitta in the Marathon Restaurant he announced his intentions to a friend known as Big Sam. "I'm going to get married!"

Sam shrugged it off. He had narrowly escaped death in three Chicago gangland wars, and nothing startled him.

"Good luck," he said. "I hope you don't crap out."

This use of a dice shooter's expression in connection with his inamorata was incongruous, but Nick forced himself to smile.

Sam read his mind. Reaching over the table, he laid one of his huge hands tenderly on Nick's shoulder. "I didn't mean nothin' bad," he apologized. "I just can't express myself like you can."

This was one time Nick didn't intend to crap out. The dice were loaded in his favor.

He was lying in bed the morning Florence was going to arrive. It was pre-dawn and his mind was spinning. He needed sleep. He wanted to be at his best on this important day, but he couldn't force her from his mind.

Sleep is something that usually comes fairly easily to the professional gambler. Upon climbing into bed he leaves his business behind—the busted flushes, the straights that won't stretch, the snake eyes and the boxcars of the dice tables begin to fade. Generally it's the staying awake—not the sleeping they can always do after the game—that's a major problem with most gamblers.

In all the cities and in all the beds in which he'd lain, nothing had gripped Nick's mind as tenaciously as Florence did now. Terrible thoughts tormented him: a train-wreck near the Continental Divide . . . the overturned cars . . . passengers crushed . . . the screaming.

He flicked the light switch and sat bolt upright. Sleep was an impossibility. He meditated on a nervous small-time safe-cracker from Cicero who once gave him his tried and proven formula for curing wakefulness: "I close my eyes and I imagines I'm twirlin' the tumblers on a bank vault. It swings open and I goes in and starts countin' money. I counts only the t'ousand buck bills. By the time I reaches about half a million, I falls asleep without no worries in the world, perfectly relaxed because I knows I got me an income for life."

Nick snapped off the light, turned the pillow over, beat it, and tried again. Instead of drifting off to sleep, he found himself at the Ziegfeld Follies. Harry Richman strutted across the stage in his high silk hat, Jack Pearl clowned through the sketches, Helen Morgan sat atop the piano singing "My Bill," and Florence came on for her number.

He remembered the stranger in the seat alongside him failing to applaud when she finished, and how he had been tempted to seize the man by the scruff of the neck, drag him up the aisle, and throw him out of the theater.

Enough flashbacks, he wearily decided. Poetry had always been a panacea for the few times he experienced insomnia. He started silently reciting, running the gamut of poets from Benet to Wordsworth. Nothing worked. Then he thought of a trump card: Elizabeth Barrett Browning's "A Child Asleep." The first few stanzas escaped his memory, but he started picking it up from there on:

> Softly, softly! Make no noises!
> Now he lieth dead and dumb;
> Now he hears the Angel's voice
> Folding silence in the room:
> Now she muses deep the meaning
> Heaven-words as they come.

The next thing he was conscious of was the ringing telephone. Mechanically he reached out, fumbled a moment, felt the instrument, and somehow managed to press the receiver against his ear.

"Yes," he mumbled sleepily.

"Good morning, sir, it's nine-thirty," said the operator all too cheerfully.

Nick said "Thanks" thickly and hung up.

His head felt woozy like a hangover, but he hadn't had one since Montreal and wasn't sure this was the way one was supposed to feel. Slowly the sleep-fog lifted from his brain, his reflexes started working, and a glorious portrait formed: Florence O'Dennison. This was to be her day and his day—the *really* important day in both their lives. They would go directly to the marriage license bureau at the City Hall and then here and there and everywhere. He would make her a present of the town, handing it to her bit by bit, to be slowly savored.

He took a long, warm shower, scrubbing every square inch of his tapering frame. From a closet in which few clothes hung he selected a double-breasted blue coat, gray flannels, black brogues, and a red-and-blue-striped necktie. There was a large patch of sunlight on the rug, which had drifted in through an open window, signifying a pleasant day, so he decided against wearing a hat.

He went down in the elevator.

"Got something good for me today, Mr. Dandolos?" the operator asked hopefully.

"Some other time," Nick said.

Entering the dining room he was ushered to a quiet table where he ordered buttered toast and a pot of coffee. His preference would have called for a Greek bread ring, oven baked, called kaluri.

He was on his second cup of coffee when Jim Devlin, a former trustworthy associate of his from Canadian racing days, dropped into the vacant chair across from him.

"Been trying to call you, Nick," he began after motioning for the waiter to bring him coffee.

"I left orders not to be disturbed," Nick replied.

"I know, that's why I came over."

"Something on your mind, Jim?"

"Yeah." He poured a little cream into his coffee. "Poker. The boys wanted me to contact you. You'd make the fifth hand. Ned Sparkman's apartment in the Beverly Wilshire Hotel."

Nick stirred his coffee absently. "Who are the others?"

"Ross Page, Rick Robinson, and Sam Renfro from Kansas City."

"I don't know Renfro," Nick said slowly, trying to place the name.

Devlin leaned across the table. "Shall I tell 'em you'll be there?"

"Sorry. Count me out."

Devlin gave a surprised whistle. "You don't want to play?"

"That's correct."

Cupping his head in his hands and resting elbows on the table, Devlin stared at Nick. "May I ask why, for the first time in his life, Nick the Greek turns down a chance to play high-stakes poker?"

"Because Nick the Greek has something more important to do."

"Name it and I'll try to believe it!"

"Marriage," Nick said.

"Marriage?"

"Yes."

"Whose?"

"Mine," Nick stated. "My girl's coming in on the train from New York. She's due at four o'clock."

Although a natural skeptic, Devlin was convinced Nick was telling the truth. He offered congratulations. After a few swallows of coffee he asked what Nick planned doing between the present and the time of the incoming train.

Nick confessed that he didn't know.

Devlin glanced at his wristwatch. "The game's going to get an early start—in about an hour," he said, and suggested, "Why don't you play a while to kill time until you go to the station?"

Nick thought it a splendid idea. He knew from years of experience that nothing murders the clock quicker than a poker game. Telephoning for his car and chauffeur, he drove to the

Beverly Wilshire Hotel in Beverly Hills. The other players were already there and he was introduced to Sam Renfro.

By the time they shook hands he didn't like him.

Renfro was small, dark, dapper. He kept pulling out a little white pocket comb and running it through his thick, greasy hair. Loud of voice, he demanded attention when he spoke and assumed the attitude that everything he said, regardless of how petty it might be, should be accepted as unquestionable gospel.

Socrates, Nick recalled, was familiar with this type of individual; he had written, "The partisan, when he is engaged in a dispute, cares nothing about the rights of the question, but is anxious only to convince his hearers of his own assertions."

Also present was Bill Keane. For years he had been treating Nick as though he was his mother, worrying over his late hours and scolding him for irregular eating habits. Bill always turned up wherever the action was; the city didn't matter. He performed the duties of a well-paid flunky, running errands and doing odd jobs. Although he was not very smart, he kept his mouth shut.

(Nick never forgot Bill's remarks one night down in Dallas after a friend of his was killed in a shooting battle. The victim was Abe Brown. Nick and Bill went to the morgue together and made positive identification. Nick gave Bill the unpleasant task of breaking the sad news to Mrs. Brown.

"Tell her gently and sympathetically," he said as he waited outside in the car.

Bill knocked on the door of the dead man's house. A woman opened it.

"Are you the Widow Brown?" Nick heard him ask in his booming voice.

"No," she replied, "I am the wife of Abe Brown."

"Five'll get you ten you're wrong," Bill said.)

When they sat down to commence play—draw poker only —Nick announced, "I've got to quit around three-fifteen."

"That's your privilege, Nick," Page said.

The players removed their coats, loosened their neckties. Nick kept his coat on, tightened his necktie. On this most significant day of his life the cards fell badly for him. By noon the best hand he had had was three jacks; but the pot was of good size, which reduced his losses to about $27,000 as they declared a fifteen-minute break for lunch.

The other players wolfed down the sandwiches. Nick dissected one, eating a small piece of ham. It was decided by mutual consent to play a solid hour of stud. Bill acted as time-keeper.

At 2:45 P.M. Jack Hanlon came in, just to kibitz. Jack was a local bookie whose tightly operated outfit maintained four telephones for bettors in different sections of the sprawling city. He had credit ratings on his customers, limiting them to a $500 maximum bet, and there wasn't a deadbeat among them. Hanlon, a handsome, forty-one-year-old bachelor, exuded healthiness, bubbled with confidence. It was rumored that his organization grossed $70,000 per day.

Precisely at three o'clock Nick lost queens and eights to three fours, and was behind almost $80,000. But by now he believed he had mastered a mannerism of the Kansas City player, and that this would give him a percentage edge.

Five minutes later only the two of them remained in a $51,000 pot. They had come to the last card. Not a pair showed. It was impossible for either to make a straight or a flush. Renfro was high on the table with a jack showing. Nick's highest card up was a ten. As a matter of fact, he had nothing higher, as he had an eight in the hole.

His eyes were glued on Renfro's face, searching for any characteristic that might furnish a key to unlock his closely guarded style of play. He found one. Renfro's little finger dug into his right ear, scratching the inside. It was a repetitive gesture. Nick remembered the last time this happened. It was when he bluffed Page out of a pot.

Renfro came out betting the size of the pot, $51,000. Counting the chips before him, Nick shoved them into the center of the table.

"You're raised another fifty-one thousand," he said.

Renfro's face turned a sickly green.

"No call," he said weakly.

As he pulled in the mountain of varicolored chips, Nick consulted his watch. It was a wristwatch he had bought a month ago and had never worn until today. It was exactly 3:15 P.M. The timing was perfect. He could just make it to the station before the train came in. He motioned for Bill to count his chips. As usual, no cash was involved in the game. Settling up would come the next day. Bill's job was to collect from the losers and carry the money to the winners.

Nick pushed his chair back and stood up. "It's been very enjoyable," he told them. Nodding good-bye, he walked toward the door, but just before his hand touched the knob his body stiffened and he halted, standing stock-still.

It was a moment of decision.

He was facing the door. Very slowly he turned and gazed longingly at the four men hunched over the card table. A sigh of resignation escaped him. Then he walked over to Jack Hanlon and asked, "Could you do me a favor?"

"Anything you say, Nick."

"Pick up my girl at the Union Station. She's coming in from New York at four o'clock. You've just got time to make it. Her name's Florence O'Dennison. Check her in at the Alexandria. A suite has been reserved in her name. Take my car and chauffeur. Tell Miss O'Dennison that I'll be around at dinner time."

Jack smiled broadly. "Be glad to, Nick, only you forgot something."

Nick asked what.

"A description of the lady."

He searched his memory. "She . . . she's beautiful," was all he could come up with.

"If she has two arms, two legs, and a head, I'll find her," Jack guaranteed, and he was off.

Nick returned to the table, sat down in the still-warm seat. "Deal me in," he said, and asked Bill to bring him a short brandy.

Page said, "You were never dealt out, Nick. We figured you couldn't leave."

Renfro, visibly shaken by his loss of the huge pot, failed to recover. His confidence was shattered. Once this happens Nick often said, it's like a man trying to walk without legs. He starts to crawl. Only losers crawl. By 5:30 P.M., out almost $400,000, Renfro muttered something unintelligible and left the apartment.

"They come . . . they go," Robinson said laconically.

Jack Hanlon came in. Nick had just folded a couple of small pairs in draw, leaving Sparkman and Robinson to battle it out, so he got up and went over to Jack.

"You certainly weren't exaggerating," Jack said enthusiastically.

"Exaggerating," Nick repeated. "About what?"

"You called her beautiful," Jack reminded him, "and that's just what she is. You're a lucky guy, Nick. All she talked about was you."

"Jack . . ."

"Yes?"

"Would it be possible for you to take Florence to dinner tonight?"

"Be a pleasure."

"And tell her I'll phone her later and see her for breakfast."

Robinson called, "It's your deal, Nick!"

He went back to the table. Two new players came in. "Fresh money," someone remarked. The game grew spirited, the cards running high. They played all night. By the time Nick got around to thinking of calling Florence it was 4:00 A.M. and he decided not to awaken her. As soon as the game broke up, which should be before noon, he would telephone and make it up to her.

Nick was behind $210,000. Page had most of the money. Bill struggled to his feet from the couch where he had been snoring heavily for the last three hours. Everyone but Nick gave him a breakfast order. Going to the kitchen, he began singing in a raucous voice and breaking eggs into a large frying pan.

After he finished serving the players, Nick went into a huddle with him and asked him to find Jack. It wouldn't be easy. Jack's activities took him to various parts of the city. When Bill did locate Jack, he was to give him a message that Nick had him repeat twice: "Use my car and chauffeur, and if you can spare the time, take Florence around as much as you can. Show her a good time. Run up any expenses you wish. I'll take care of all the tabs."

During the middle of the afternoon Bill came in and whispered in his ear, "It's all settled, Mr. Nick. Mr. Jack says he'll take care of Miss O'Dennison until the game's over."

Nick slipped him a $100 bill.

"Mr. Nick . . ." he began.

"I know, Bill," Nick said, interpreting his thoughts, "you want me to quit."

"Tonight. Don't ruin your health."

"We'll see, Bill."

Play continued throughout the day. At midnight Nick was on the hook for just under $375,000. No one wanted to quit, least of all he.

Again they played all night.

Bill approached Nick the next morning. "You look kinda tired, Mr. Nick."

"Never felt better," Nick answered, lighting a fresh cigar and taking a sip of orange juice.

Bill suggested gently, "You oughta stop soon."

"I may just do that, Bill," Nick placated him.

"When you're ready I'll drive you home in my car."

He wasn't ready. A hundred hands and a new day, and they were still at it. Bill went out for a bottle of Metaxas brandy for Nick and downtown to his hotel room for three boxes of cigars—just in case the game continued. During the night Nick had bluffed his way through two nice pots and had drawn two full houses and a queen-high straight in others. By morning he had cut his losses in half.

New players arrived and old players left. Only Ross Page, Rick Robinson, Ned Sparkman, and Nick remained of the original starters. At the end of the fourth day they were still at it. Nick hadn't telephoned Florence, but he managed to get another message through to Jack Hanlon to keep on entertaining her and that he would call her the first chance he had.

That chance didn't seem to come.

Bill was hounding Nick harder. "Your heart won't stand it," he repeated endlessly.

Nick leaned back into the chair that had almost become part of his body, and dealt mechanically. He hadn't gone to the bathroom for twelve straight hours. He often said, "Going to the bathroom during a poker or dice game is a mistake. You might miss a hot hand worth a hundred thousand, and nothing in the bathroom is worth that much."

In the last twelve hours he had cut his losses $75,000. It would be tough sledding to get even, but the cards seemed to be running better, and with a few breaks, a measure of luck, and a modicum of skill it could be done.

The fifth day and night went by. His body and hands felt numb, and when dealing he just seemed to spin the cards out with a reflex action. His mind, though, was clear. And Bill kept relentlessly working on him, trying to persuade him to quit and go to bed.

"It isn't worth it, Mr. Nick," Bill argued. "Think it over. A man's heart can take just so much."

By now Florence had slipped from his mind, inundated by the undiminishing stream of card consciousness. Along toward midafternoon of the sixth day, he staged a fine rally, winning five consecutive pots. It was a splendid comeback, allowing him to get virtually even.

It was at this juncture that Sparkman posed a general question: "Anybody thinking of quitting?"

None bothered to answer.

Nick noticed Sparkman's facial coloring. He had a frightening pallor. Despite the pleasant temperature of the apartment, tiny globules of perspiration gathered on his forehead. The dampness of brow brought to mind a poem of Longfellow's:

> His brow is wet with honest sweat,
> He earns whate'er he can,
> And looks the whole world in the face
> For he owes not any man.

He asked Sparkman solicitously, "You feel alright, Ned?"

"Sure." The host smiled feebly, mopping at his damp brow with a white silk handkerchief, and remarked, "It's a great night for poker."

It certainly was a great night for Nick the Greek. By morning of the seventh day of nonstop action, after playing catch-up during the entire session, Nick was blithely sailing along in front, the winds of luck pushing at this back. Roughly figuring, he was ahead half a million.

It was a tough game. Page, Robinson, and Sparkman were old pros, not cut from the ordinary cloth of poker players. They were cool, efficient, calculating, crafty, ruthless. They knew when to fold, and they knew when to make their chips talk. It was impossible to read them accurately, to detect a flaw as Nick had with Renfro. Compared with them, the man from Kansas City was a rank amateur with a puffed-up ego, stepping out of his class.

Like all professionals, Page, Robinson, and Sparkman parlayed poor pots and smart play to better-than-average success. There was an iciness about them, and a coyness. They'd use routines: show nervousness on lousy hands, calmness on good ones. Then switch routines. Figuring their moves was comparable to breaking a secret wartime code, but periodically, coupled with guesswork and patience, Nick felt he could do it to some extent.

Play slowed considerably during the seventh day. Everyone but Nick made frequent lavatory trips to splash cool water on his face. Robinson folded a handkerchief around some ice cubes, pressed them against his cheeks and the nape of his neck. Someone else took a soft drink bottle from the icebox and held the side of it first against one closed eye, then the other. After accidentally getting a drop of water on a card—to the consternation of the players—Robinson discontinued his resuscitation system.

They called for a fresh deck of cards and Bill brought one to the table. It was the sixty-fourth used thus far.

Bill kept nagging Nick. "You're committing suicide. The human heart can't take this abuse. You've gotta go home."

"When the boys are ready to break it up, I'm ready," he said.

After a full seven days and nights, plus eight additional hours, Page mumbled tiredly, "Another couple of hours and that's all I can take." He glanced around the table.

All the players except Nick agreed on a two-hour time limit. They turned their heavy-lidded eyes on him, and Sparkman asked, "What about you?" Seldom did losers want a winner to quit.

He shrugged and said, "I'll go along with the majority."

The game had forty minutes to run when there was a knock on the door. Bill opened it cautiously. A bellboy was holding a yellow envelope in his hand.

"Is Mr. Nick Dandolos here?"

"I'll take it," Bill said.

He brought the telegram to the table and laid it down alongside Nick's towering piles of chips. Nick, who had just won the pot, putting him approximately $680,000 ahead, raked it in, stacked the chips. Then he ripped open the telegram and read:

FLORENCE AND I MARRIED IN MEXICO TODAY. WE BOTH LOVE YOU.

JACK

"Something the matter, Nick?" Page inquired.

Nick didn't answer. He kept reading the wire over and over again. Page twice more repeated the question.

For the first time Page's words penetrated the mental blockade, and Nick answered, "No, nothing's wrong that a strong dose of philosophy won't cure," but the words sounded hollow.

He reread the telegram once more and, tearing it into small pieces, placed them neatly in his ashtray. Then he began playing in a style that was in marked contrast to his usual game; he displayed an absolute contempt for percentages. He was daring, reckless, erratic.

From that moment on until the end of the game—thirty-eight minutes later—Nick raised and raised and raised. It mattered not whether he even had a pair. He virtually handed back every cent he was ahead, plus an additional quarter of a million dollars!

The other players made no comment. It seemed to be an off-season visit from Santa Claus. Robinson, Page, and Sparkman, who knew him well, realized something drastic had happened in his life. The others were unaware of this. Rumors would start flying in the morning that Nick the Greek had gone berserk.

"Come on, Mr. Nick," faithful Bill coaxed. "I'll drive you home."

He drove him to the Alexandria. As he was getting out of the car, Nick said, "Come around in about eight hours." He planned that when he woke up he would dig up the money to pay off his markers, which Bill would deliver.

"You take care of yourself, Mr. Nick," Bill said. "You don't look too good."

Nick shut the car door. "Thanks, Bill, see you later," he promised.

Bill didn't answer.

Nick looked at him. His head was turned sideways, resting against the steering wheel. His mouth was stiff and open, as if in paralysis. The one eye visible had a glassy appearance.

Nick sprinted into the hotel lobby. "Get a doctor and ambulance, fast!" he ordered the startled desk clerk.

Although he had no way of knowing then, speed was unimportant. The doctor told him later that death from a coronary was instantaneous.

And Bill had been worrying about Nick's heart!

When Nick finally reached his room he was exhausted. He undressed, and fatigued as he was, hung his clothes neatly in the closet. He opened the door a few inches, then climbed into bed. He reached for the telephone and asked that a bellboy be sent up. Jimmy arrived. He had done a few things for Nick in the past. Nick handed him a fifty dollar bill. "Get me a girl," he requested.

Jimmy carefully folded the money, tucking it into a hip pocket. "Any preference?" he wanted to know. "Blonde, brunette, redhead?" He waited for Nick to make a choice.

Nick closed his eyes, and into his mind came a detailed physical picture of Florence, so clear that he wondered if, during the years ahead, it would ever fade. With great exactitude he detailed what he desired in the appearance of the woman he wished Jimmy to bring him.

Everything about her was the exact opposite of Florence O'Dennison.

Twenty minutes went by. He waited in bed, the door unlocked. There was a knock and he called, "Come in!"

She came into the room. Her hair was a dull, mousy color and she wore too much makeup, the mascara caked heavily. She walked over to the bed on feet that were probably tired from years of pavement pounding in search of customers, and said, "My name's Norma. I'll show you a good time, honey."

She started to undress.

"Hold it!" Nick called.

The girl paused and regarded him quizzically.

"Keep your clothes on, Norma."

"Say! What is . . ."

"Listen to me," Nick interrupted. He pointed to a chair alongside his bed. "You just sit down here and read a magazine, or think, or whatever you want to do. Watch the clock on the bureau. Wake me up once every hour. Just once, understand? Every time you wake me I'll give you a hundred dollars."

She stared at him with widening eyes.

"At the end of eight hours," Nick continued, "you can leave. And thanks."

She moved to the edge of the bed, wondering if she had heard correctly. After all the unusual demands men had made on her, this simple one topped them all.

"That's all I have to do to earn eight hundred dollars?"

"That's all, Norma."

She laughed delightedly. It was the only time she could remember laughing spontaneously while on a job.

A quotation from Lord Byron came into Nick's tired and troubled mind:

> And if I laugh at any mortal thing,
> 'tis that I may not weep.

Norma asked, "When do we start?"

"Right now," Nick said, stretching out and turning on his side away from her. "See you in an hour."

"With a hundred dollars," she reminded.

"Right under my pillow, waiting for you," he told her.

What he didn't tell her, and had never told a soul, was about his only fear in life. Perhaps it was a quirk, a phobia, possibly an intuition—he couldn't explain the motivation. But he knew of the fear that always haunted him when he was exhausted as he was now. If he slept too many hours in a stretch he might never wake up again.

He couldn't rely on night telephone operators or desk clerks to call him, nor on alarm clocks. Women of a so-called low station in life—such as Norma—were, he believed, more reliable. They were thankful for the easy money, and their minds came so alive with thoughts of what they might buy with it that to doze off was out of the question.

Just before he fell asleep he thought of tomorrow. Tomorrow would be a light day. Only two items were on his agenda: a visit to several safe deposit vaults for money to pay off his losses, and making necessary burial arrangements for Bill.

Long Live the King!

"GAMBLERS, with but few exceptions, are the most honest men in the world."

Nick often reiterated this statement, qualifying it by maintaining that individual gamblers were scrupulously trustworthy, but the same wasn't always true of gambling joint operators.

For the gambler himself—to whom it was a livelihood—his word was his bond, and that, in Nick's opinion, was worth twice the assurances of the average businessman. The gambler's entire career hinged on reliability, and if temptations to cheat should tug at him, they were quickly overcome. To the men who lived by the Wheel of Fortune, an unimpeachable reputation was a commodity that money could not buy.

When mutual trust between members of the gambling fraternity was discussed, Nick would cite the time a bored millionaire Texas gambler, Blondie Hall, telephoned him long distance in Las Vegas.

Hall proposed, "You flip a coin and I'll call it, for ten grand."

Nick tossed a quarter into the air, catching it on the back of his hand. "Call it," he told Hall.

"Heads," Hall said.

It was tails.

"You lose," Nick said.

"Okay," Hall replied. "Send you a check tomorrow." And he hung up.

The honesty of palatial gambling casinos such as those fronting the Las Vegas Strip and others to be found downtown in that same city or in Reno or Tahoe is impeccable. It isn't necessary to rig any of the games when percentages are working for the owners.

In the joints, or lower-class places which once flourished, a customer could take a good clipping. Some used an electric current, controlled at will on the dice table or roulette wheel. Nick applied an unfailing test in these shady spots. When suspicious, he dropped a steel key on the table at a time when he suspected the magnetic current might be turned on.

"If the key remains flat and doesn't move, the house is honest," Nick contended. "If it goes through any gyrations, a man should grab his hat and leave."

On one occasion Nick himself was indirectly accused of cheating by a sore loser. Playing poker with six motion-picture-studio bigwigs, he enjoyed a phenomenal streak of luck, winning virtually all the money. Rumor reached him the next day that one of the players had remarked that a person would have to be dishonest to beat everyone the way Nick had.

He went to the studio to see the man who had cast aspersions upon his name. He was a producer who, as nearly as Nick could ascertain, had lost $6,300 in the game.

Nick dropped the money on his desk with the warning, "You had better be careful with your false accusations."

The producer's face blanched. Nick walked out.

Dice, Nick said, were introduced into America by a Frenchman named Louis Philippe, while on a visit to New Orleans. Negroes around the bayous and levees were the first to popularize it to any extent. Within a short time the game spread to all corners of the nation.

Before Nick made his everlasting contribution to the game by giving it a touch of elegance, cheating was rampant and it was an easy matter to find a crooked sporting goods manufacturer willing to sell dice that, according to the instruction manual, were "guaranteed to win."

Quicksilver and amalgam were used to load the dice. However, the dice sometimes became detectable because mercury —a heavy, silver-white metallic element, the only metal that is liquid at ordinary temperatures—worked through the pores of the cubes, causing discoloration. The result could become fatal to the user, for an irate loser, who now had positive proof of being cheated, sometimes gained his revenge with the aid of a knife or gun. If lucky, the deceiver came out of it with only bruises and contusions.

The price of crooked dice ranged from five to fifteen dollars per pair. They were made of vegetable ivory, ivory celluloid, bone, and a composition called zyle. The human eye could find nothing wrong with them. They felt the same in the hand, and their weight was identical with that of honest dice. In transparent dice the metal was concealed in the spots.

There were twenty-six accepted ways to throw the dice in your favor, whether by hand or from a dice box. Manufacturers made extravagant but somewhat true claims when their advertising contended, "We can teach you to make your point whether on a hard or a soft surface." They also asserted they could educate you to throw seven or eleven any time when "coming out," and to prevent throwing craps.

A number of foreign countries tried to install dice layouts, but they failed to catch on. Only England in the present "Swinging London Days" has succeeded in giving them the "American touch." The French failed completely after extensive research. During the 1957 season when the world-famous Monte Carlo Casino found that, due to heavy expenses and the fading popularity of roulette, they were in the red, the management decided to introduce "*les craps.*"

Two of their executives came to the United States to study the game. Among those consulted was Nick the Greek. They visited a number of gambling houses, soaking up the atmosphere. After four months they brought back their knowledge of the game, accompanied by tape recordings of the players' screams of joy when a point was made.

"I am certain," Nick remarked, "that it took them a long time to figure out 'Baby Needs New Shoes.' "

Despite their advance studying and planning, there were incongruities when they opened several dice tables at Monte Carlo. For one thing, the vocabulary of the stickmen sounded different. The feverishness of the players seemed missing, Somehow the Continental touch wasn't applicable to the spotted cubes.

A friend of Nick's dissuaded him from going to Prince Rainier country to try his luck. "You could win millions of francs and not get any thrill," he informed Nick. That cooled him off. If there was no thrill, it was certain there would be no Nick.

It is the considered opinion of a vast majority of gamblers that Nick was responsible for the installation of crap tables in a multiplicity of toney places. High society that normally wouldn't be caught slumming in such surroundings stormed in to watch the dapper Greek play.

Most of them were astounded to learn that the highest rolling professional free-lance gambler in the history of the world possessed a vocabulary containing words of more syllables than were to be found in "call" or "raise," and was fluently conversant in a number of languages.

Nick did not bemoan, nor was he dismayed by, the fact that the public rarely thinks of a gambler as a man of culture. "Most of them aren't," was his contention, and he added, "If you tried to discuss art with any of them and mentioned a painting of 'The Last Supper,' the majority would think you were referring to something they'd eaten that evening."

One night Nick was gambling at the Sands Hotel in Las Vegas, stooping slightly over the green felt table, waiting to see if he had won or lost $5,000 he had bet against the roller of the dice making his point, when he felt a tug on his sleeve. Turning, he looked into the soft face of a pretty tourist whose eyes held the innocent look of the cherries on a slot machine.

She whispered, "Sir, which one is Nick the Greek?"

"I believe, my dear, that is a sobriquet with which they have tagged me," Nick replied.

She backed away two feet, peering at him in amazement, while her mind grappled with the meaning of "sobriquet." She decided to try again.

"Are *you* the famous Nick the Greek who has won millions of dollars?"

"Yes," Nick admitted, "and also lost millions."

"Wow!" she exclaimed, eyes popping. "Why, you're a bigger attraction than Boulder Dam!"

Nick bowed before her, and swung around to the table—in synchronization with the roller making his point, an eight, and the stick man scooping up his chips and calling, "Coming out with the next shooter!"

He laid down another large bet against the dice.

Behind him he heard the girl talking to a friend, and caught a fragment of the conversation. "Yes, Cathy, it's *really* Nick the Greek. He just confirmed it. He's not at all like I supposed he'd be. Why, his manners are positively princely."

A magazine writer, Robin Harris, neatly summarized the results of his many appearances at the gaming tables: "If he never did another thing, The Greek made a lasting contribution to Americana by lifting the dice game to its present eminence."

During the years following Harris' judgment Nick did

many more things that will live forever in the minds of numerous people. But perhaps his most important opportunity for immortality outside the gambling world, he muffed.

Back in 1927 no American had yet flown the Atlantic Ocean in a solo flight. During this period Nick was headquartering in New Orleans, eating his fill of oysters on the half shell, which he loved, and losing nightly in gambling. It was here that he bumped into Dick Merrill, a mail route aviator who had read of a prize offered by New York hotel owner Raymond Orteig to anyone flying alone across the Atlantic. The prize was $25,000.

"I can do it," Merrill told Nick, "but I need financing. It'll take thirty thousand dollars, and I'll cut you in on half of everything I make." He was sure the amount he mentioned was petty cash to the Greek.

Nick said that he didn't think that $25,000 was much inducement for a man to fly solo over a lot of lonely water.

"But it isn't the prize money alone," Merrill pointed out. "Think of the additional revenue from personal appearances, movies, the writing of a book, endorsements, and so on. The aggregate will be many thousands. And if you put up the money, you're a partner and share in the fame."

Nick mulled it over. "There'd be some stipulations."

Merrill asked him to name them.

"No mention that I'm the backer of this enterprise, and under no circumstances is my name to go into any book. You take full credit."

Merrill agreed, asking, "Is it a deal, then?"

"It's a deal."

"Great!" Merrill exulted. In his mind he was already landing in France.

"As soon as I raise the money," Nick said.

The flier was stunned. "You mean you don't have thirty thousand dollars?" he asked incredulously.

Nick reached into his pocket, fished out some bills. He had about $1,400. "You know how it is with a gambler," he shrugged. "Here today . . . gone tomorrow."

Merrill was crestfallen.

"But don't worry," the flier was reassured. "I'll do my level best to get it for you."

"When?" Merrill was impatient. It was rumored that others might attempt the ocean flying feat.

"I said, 'Here today . . . gone tomorrow,'" Nick repeated. "I said nothing about tonight. The Colonial Inn. Faro."

"Not craps or roulette?" Merrill said questioningly. He didn't understand faro.

Nick shook his head. "Faro's the best bet. You get almost an even break with the house." He rattled off some additional odds. "With dice it's 1.03 to 1. Against the twenty-one player it's 1.06 to 1. Roulette is the roughest game to buck. Even betting red or black, or odd or even, the house holds a big edge of 1.11 to 1."

By now Merrill's hopes were airborne. He had examined and test driven all the planes capable of flying the Atlantic, and had decided on a Ryan monoplane. Nick's money would buy him that plane.

For two straight nights at the Colonial Inn Nick played faro with a nervous, eager, and expectant Dick Merrill standing over his chair. Gradually the $1,400 rose to $30,000.

"We've got it!" Merrill exclaimed jubilantly. "I'll leave for St. Louis in the morning and buy the plane."

Nick suggested they have dinner and talk it over. The food at the Colonial was fit for a king, so they went into the beautifully appointed dining room. Merrill began talking of aeronautics, and in Nick he had a fascinated listener as he described in detail what might be expected on the dangerous pioneer flight to Europe, from tricky head winds to chartings and unexpected storms.

"There seems to have been much progress since the abortive effort of Darius Green and His Flying Machine," Nick said with tongue in cheek.

Merrill hardly heard him. Dreams of fame and fortune were flying through his head.

On the way out it was necessary to pass by the gambling casino. Glancing in at the action, Nick halted. "Dick," he said, "a man must always prepare for the unexpected. As of now we have just about enough money, but unanticipated expenses may crop up."

He paused.

"No," Merrill protested, a ripple of fear running through him. "I figured it to the last penny. We have enough." He was a practical man.

Nick started for the faro table. Wild horses couldn't have stopped him. Over his shoulder he called to a nervous Merrill, "I'll get just a few thousand extra to put you on the safe side."

Nick played all night, and as the first gray streaks of dawn appeared over New Orleans he lost his last dollar and Merrill lost his chance to be the first to fly the Atlantic. He tried to comfort the flier by quoting William McFee: "If fate means you to lose, give him a good fight anyhow"; and he concluded, with a pat on Merrill's back, "We gave them a good fight, didn't we, Dick?"

In the state of deep disappointment the flier nodded absently. He couldn't have cared less about the philosophy of William McFee. All he knew was that his once-in-a-lifetime chance had slipped away.

The next day Nick lolled in one of the oyster houses, sighted a gambler he knew, and borrowed the fare back to California. Merrill returned to his old job of handling a mail plane. Three weeks later Charles A. Lindbergh flew the Atlantic and became a national hero. Some years later—though by this time flying to Europe was old hat—Merrill made the flight with Harry Richman, the musical comedy star, plus thousands of ping pong balls carried as ballast.

Back in his bailiwick of Los Angeles, Nick went on a winning streak. The East Coast had proven unlucky. The West Coast was just the opposite. "I could fall down a steep flight of stairs, pick up a thousand dollar bill on the last step, and land on my feet unhurt out here," he said.

In the past he had made considerable sums of money betting on his friend Jack Dempsey. The only setback occurred when Dempsey tangled with Gene Tunney in Philadelphia in 1926 and lost the heavyweight championship. Nick had gone to Atlantic City to watch Dempsey train and believed the fight to be only a workout. He hadn't counted on Tunney's speed, footwork, and pure boxing ability, and he was out $190,000 when the referee raised the ex-Marine's hand in victory.

He boarded a train for New York with his pal Mike Lyman, a man who had ambitions to become a restauranteur. From Los Angeles to New York and then to Philadelphia was a long, tiresome train ride, and to pass the time Nick proposed to Mike that they try their hand at some game of chance.

"I only play bridge," Mike informed him.

Nick said, "You would pick the only game I don't know."

Mike offered to teach him. At the conclusion of a two-hour instructional period, Nick said he was ready for a game, and proposed a modest cent a point.

Lyman grinned and said, "I'd like to accommodate you, but I'm busted. I've got barely enough money for the trip."

Nick was not about to pass up any action. "I'll extend you fifteen hundred dollars credit."

"The price is right," Lyman said. "Cut you for deal."

The first day Nick won $80.00.

Next day the stakes were doubled and Lyman won $2,600. On the third day they played for $8.00 per point, then raised it to $12.00 for the remainder of the trip.

By the time the pair reached New York City, Lyman was

$240,000 ahead. Nick unstrapped a suitcase and counted out 240 thousand dollar bills, which he handed to his fellow traveler. Lyman nearly fainted. He had expected the Greek to settle for a few thousand. The Dempsey–Tunney fight in Philadelphia had suddenly become unimportant to him. At last he could fulfill his dreams and get into the restaurant business.

Inadvertently, Nick had become his backer.

Mike took the first train back to Los Angeles. With his older brother, Abe Simon he purchased a Hill Street restaurant called Herbert's, changing the name to Lyman's. For his maitre d' he hired Joe Mann, who had a large following. The waiters were oldtimers, mostly German, who took a fatherly interest in the customers. If they didn't approve of something on the menu, they advised against ordering it.

One evening Nick dropped into Lyman's for a cheeseburger. The waiter, recognizing him, asked if he had enjoyed it.

"Pretty tasty," Nick said, "but hardly worth two hundred forty thousand dollars."

He told Lyman, "You'd better serve good food here, or indirectly I'll carry it on my conscience that I poisoned thousands."

Lyman joked, "Come in any time, Nick, and have a cup of coffee on me."

Mike Lyman became a millionaire.

For the first time Nick bet against Dempsey in his return tiff. Tunney won. This was the fight featured by the famous "long count." Dempsey received $300,000 for his share, and Nick remarked, "I got the same amount with no exercise."

As his bankroll grew healthier, Nick's mind dwelt on a single purpose: again to pit his wits, skill and money against Arnold Rothstein. He wanted the honor—if such it could be called—of being the top gambler in the United States. He wanted it so badly it gnawed at him. At present he was resting unhappily in the number-two slot. He resolved to do something to reverse the positions. He traveled the ninety miles from Philadelphia to New York. This time he wouldn't rush into a game, but planned to acclimate himself more to the big city. When the time seemed propitious, he would tackle his nemesis.

Although he saw Rothstein every day, he turned down several invitations to gamble. He was working himself up to a mood. He was tired of hearing Rothstein's name continually mentioned as the leading gambler in the world; and his intentions were to push him off the mythical throne. And soon.

He was sure he could do it.

The fact that he wasn't playing against Rothstein didn't mean that the Greek was out of the action. Far from it. There was a game awaiting him almost every night if he so desired. One nice balmy evening he was standing in front of Lindy's. At his feet a shine boy was putting a high gloss on his dark shoes. Billy Rose, the impresario, strolled up to him.

"What's doing tonight, Nick?" Rose asked.

"There's a game across the street from Macy's," Nick disclosed.

Rose said, "I'll ask a foolish question: Are you going to play?"

Nick answered in the affirmative. He tossed the shoeshine boy double or nothing, won, and still gave the youngster a quarter.

"Mind if I tag along?" Rose questioned.

"Delighted to have you, Billy."

They walked south on Broadway, jostled by the crowds leaving the theaters. The location of the game called for nearly a ten-block walk. Nick enjoyed walking and watching "the passing show," as he termed it. Closely scrutinizing pedestrians, he would try to guess their businesses.

"Once I made a bet that a certain man on the street was an important business executive," Nick related. "He carried a cane, wore a Chesterfield overcoat and a Homburg. I asked him his business. He said, 'Barber.' ' "

Billy Rose posed a general question as to what Nick had been doing lately. Nick replied that he had been reading Algernon Charles Swinburne, the English poet.

"I can't place him," Rose said.

"I can refresh you," Nick offered.

"Please do," Rose said.

No request could have been better fulfilled. Nick started reciting, and Rose, walking alongside of him, their steps in cadence, listened. As they neared Macy's Nick concluded with:

> We are not sure of sorrow
> and joy was never sure.
> Today will die tomorrow;
> Time stoops to no man's lure;
> And love, grown faint and fretful,
> With lips but half regretful
> Sighs, and with eyes forgetful
> Weeps that no loves endure.

They paused at the doorway of an old loft building. An unsavory character who was chewing tobacco while holding a toothpick in the side of his mouth looked them over and nodded to the man running the elevator. Taken to the third floor, they went through a metal fire door into a room where, around a billiard table, a floating crap game operated by O. K. Coakley was in progress. The ceiling was low, the room huge. Players were clustered three deep around the table.

They made room for Nick.

As usual, Nick was betting against the dice. The shooter who was coming out was an actor, and when he hit his eleventh pass Nick turned away from the table.

"See you again, gentlemen, and thank you," were his parting words.

He walked to the elevator with Rose.

"If it's not too personal, how much did you lose?" Rose inquired.

"Oh, I'm not sure," Nick returned, "but I'd guess it was in the neighborhood of two hundred forty thousand dollars."

Rose whistled sharply. "That's a rather expensive neighborhood."

Nick changed the subject. "Do you know much about painting, Billy?"

"Lips, houses, or canvases?"

"Canvases. Oils."

Rose said, "I've got a pretty valuable collection, including a Rembrandt."

"Rembrandt," Nick repeated, his interest quickening. "I was studying an alleged Rembrandt yesterday at the Metropolitan Museum. It was called 'Old Lady Cutting Her Fingernails.' "

Rose acknowledged that he had heard of it.

"Well," Nick continued, "there seems to be some doubt, the art experts claim, of its authenticity. Many ascribe it to Nicolaes Maas, popularly known as Maes. I can understand the existing doubts. Maas, like Rembrandt, was a Dutchman. Rembrandt was twenty-six years older than Maas and greatly influenced his style—as did Van Dyck."

Rose did a double take and shook his head wonderingly. Here was a man who had just lost close to a quarter of a million dollars, seemingly putting the matter out of his mind and discussing art like a connoisseur.

"Anyway," Nick concluded, "no matter who actually painted it, this is a minor masterpiece."

When they reached Nick's hotel, the Alamac, Nick suggested that Rose come up for a nightcap. Rose accepted. The Greek's room was near the top floor, small and cool. By his bed, Rose noted, was a plate containing an orange. He then trained his eyes on Nick's face. A man just couldn't lose that amount of money, he kept thinking, without an angry blowup about it.

Suddenly he saw Nick frown and exclaim, "Dammit!"

This is it, Rose surmised. All the pent-up suppressions and repressions that have been burning within him since suffering the staggering loss are reaching the surface. No one, he reasoned, could lose that much money without a violent explosion.

He knew his assumptions were correct when he saw Nick pick up a desk chair and hurl it across the room where it smashed into the wall.

Going to the telephone, Nick jerked it off the hook and shouted at the operator, "Give me the manager!" His voice was hard and threatening. Fifteen seconds later he shouted, "McKelway, when I checked into this place I had a standing order that an orange and a banana were to be sent to my room each night. Well, the orange is here, no doubt of that—but the banana is missing."

He paused, listened for a few moments, then said, "I'll accept your deduction that the night maid ate it, but if you'd pay your help more so they could eat decently, this wouldn't happen to inconvenience the guests."

He hung up.

Turning to Rose, the man who had lost enough money to buy a good portion of a banana plantation in a Central American country was flushed with joy. "They're sending the banana right up," he chortled.

He isn't human, Rose thought. He thinks of a banana instead of money.

Nick began seeing Rothstein every day. Often they lunched together. Nick had heard Rothstein referred to (but never to his face) as "The Brain," "The Bankroll," "The Man Upstairs," "Banker to the Underworld." To Nick he was just plain Arnold, and of him he said, "Arnold wasn't a bad guy. He had lots of nice qualities. He wasn't a well man and his memory was faulty and getting progressively worse. He'd tell you something and an hour later would forget what he told you."

One night Rothstein lost $350,000 in a poker game. At least two players held his markers for the full amount. He told Nick, "I'm not going to pay up."

Nick asked why.

"Because I was cheated," Rothstein said. He failed to elaborate on this and Nick did not question him.

"Arnold," Nick advised, "you better pay off." He reminded him, "You were playing with some pretty tough boys."

Rothstein answered cockily, "I'm pretty tough myself."

Nick kept worrying about Rothstein not paying off. His thoughts were not one hundred percent altruistic. When pressed, he admitted his concern stemmed partially from the fact that he didn't want anything to happen to Rothstein's health until he settled several old scores over the poker table.

On Sunday noon of November 4, 1929, Nick telephoned Rothstein at the Park Central Hotel, where the gambling king resided, and made an appointment to meet him at Lindy's Restaurant at 10:00 P.M.

"I want to have a long talk with you, Arnold," Nick said, "and I think you know what it is about." He didn't want to discuss it over the telephone.

"I'll meet you," was Rothstein's reply.

That evening Nick took a showgirl from the Bandbox Revue to dinner and a movie afterwards. The movie was *Underworld*, written by Ben Hecht. Nick had always been a cinema lover, and he become so engrossed in this particular picture, he discovered he was half an hour late for his Rothstein appointment.

He went to Lindy's with the showgirl—to learn that Rothstein had been waiting for him but had left to go to his hotel. Nick felt bad. It was one of the few times in his life he had failed to be on time. Knowing that Rothstein often went to bed early, he decided to wait until morning to call and apologize.

It was a call that would never be made.

Nick and the girl had just finished their late supper when Abe Scher, the night cashier, came over to the table and announced, "Nick, I've got some bad news to tell you."

Nick sensed what it was.

Scher informed him, "Arnold Rothstein was shot about half an hour ago in the Park Central. The bullet hit him in the abdomen. He's in Polyclinic Hospital."

"What are his chances?"

"According to my informant, it wouldn't be a good bet to take that he'll recover," Scher answered.

Early the following morning Detective Patrick Flood entered Rothstein's hospital room and pulled a chair up to the bed. Rothstein's eyes were closed, but hearing the movement, he opened them, recognizing the caller.

"Hello, Patty," he said. His face was chalk white and his eyes were large brown holes.

Flood said, "Hello, Arnold. Who shot you?"

The question was a mere formality. Flood expected no revelation.

"I won't talk," Rothstein said, adding, "I'll take care of it myself, Patty."

The detective stood up. "Get well, Arnold," he said, and left the room. Outside, a dozen reporters surrounded him. "He told me nothing," was all he had for them.

Rothstein died.

His empire of vice was taken over by Frank Costello. Rothstein's operations had been limited to New York City. Costello expanded. He had no boundaries. His dope and bookmaking rackets extended all the way to California, a territory given to Bugsy Siegel.

Yes, the King of the Gamblers was dead—and long live the new King, Nicholas Andrea Dandolos, an educated gentleman from Crete who played for thrills and not mere money.

The Battered Suitcase

NICHOLAS Dandolos reigned as undisputed gambling monarch of the world from 1928 until 1949. He was dethroned in 1949, forced into abdication by percentages, a dwindling of high-stakes games (particularly in New York City where civic-minded Mayor Fiorello LaGuardia, "The Little Flower," who bloomed from 1934 until 1945, clamped down on big-time gambling), and a body blow suffered in 1949 at a Las Vegas poolside lowball poker game. He went to Federal Court to prove he was bilked out of $550,000. He lost the case. He also lost his magic ability to tap the pure gold vein of credit.

"You can't beat death, taxes, and percentages," was an oft-repeated aphorism of Nick's. He compared percentages to an unscalable wall. "Percentages are sticklers for the truth," he asserted. "They never lie. If you get one percent the worst of it now, you'll still get the worst of it a hundred years from now. Two and two make four today, and will still add up to four a hundred million years from today. The logic of percentages makes arguments to the contrary useless."

But during this twenty-one-year reign he was recognized as the Supreme Being of Gambling by all—from penny pitchers to house-limit bettors—and the predators, the pretenders, the Johnny-come-latelies, and the fish-eyed veteran pros never had to stalk their intended prey, Nick the Greek. No matter how elaborate his plans for the evening might be, a telephone call was sufficient to flush him out. They came for a run at him, equipped with the necessary requisites: money and good credit ratings. They eventually left, an hour or a few days latter —stripped of everything. The Greek showed them no mercy. He was a Triton among minnows.

He became the chief arbiter in gambling disputes, the recipient of many long distance telephone calls for rulings on the fine points upon which a bet might hinge. His decisions were accepted with the validity of an edict from the higher courts.

His influence was widespread; his name became a household one. Winners of penny-ante poker games were often kidded by comparisons to Nick the Greek. A New Jersey hood who told his wife, "I ain't buyin' you no mink coat, baby," received a bawling out from the little woman. "Why can't you talk like Nick the Greek, a gentleman? He'd say, 'I'm *not* buyin' you no fur coat, baby.'"

During his lush years Nick maintained a penthouse atop the Beverly Wilshire Hotel, used primarily for entertainment purposes and a loanout to servicemen during World War II. He contended he felt "more comfortable" in a single sleeping room.

It seemed natural that the theatrical crowd would adopt him as one of their favorite sons, and he enjoyed lasting friendships with Louis B. Mayer, boss of Metro-Goldwyn-Mayer, Carl Laemmle, owner of Universal Studios, Joseph M. Schenck, head of Fox Studio; agents Eddie Mannix, Frank Orsatti, and Lou Irwin; actors Clark Gable, W. C. Fields, Harpo Marx, John Barrymore, George Raft, and Mickey Rooney; entertainers Frank Sinatra and Joe E. Lewis; actresses Ava Gardner, Constance Bennett, Clara Bow, and Billie Dove;

playwright-producer-writer-director George M. Cohan; impresario Mike Todd; Tallulah Bankhead, Irving Berlin, Enrico Caruso, and Aristotle Onassis.

While socializing with them, he often expounded on theories for character building. "Giving up something you seem hooked on is comparatively simple," he would say, "if you remove the temptation. This diminishes the resistance, but doesn't do much to strengthen your character.

"The real character-building test comes from close proximity to the forbidden. I've tried it three times and conquered it three times. I once went on a milk diet for a week, advised to do so by a doctor. This cleans up my system and regulates my weight. While on this fasting kick I'll take a friend out to dinner each evening and watch him devour a full-course meal, and even though it nearly kills me, I'll sit across from him and only sip milk.

"Then I had a sore throat. Nothing serious, but it was suggested that I lay off cigars for a while. This I did successfully —after making it a point to be in smoke-filled rooms close to other cigar smokers.

"Also I bet five hundred dollars I could stand in the middle of the Sands Hotel casino and not make a bet for two hours.

"At the conclusion of these experiments my weight was down, my system cleaned out, my throat well, and my character immeasurably strengthened."

He neglected to mention that the moment his friend handed him a five hundred dollar bill in the Sands casino, signifying he had won his bet, he rushed to the crap table and bet it on "don't pass."

He enjoyed hobnobbing with intellectuals, and on one occasion at Berkeley he found himself the target of questions hurled by probing University of California professors, assistant professors, and instructors determined to explore the inexplicable Greek. Here is a partial list of these, with his answers:

PROFESSORS: Could you give up gambling completely?

NICK: Any time I wish.

PROFESSORS: What's the most important thing to a gambler?

NICK: That's rather a general question, but let me put it this way: In Boston, it's How much does he know? In New York, it's How much is he worth? In Philadelphia, it's Who were his parents? In gambling, it's Is he good for his markers?

PROFESSORS: Do you ever regret not taking a legitimate job when you were young—one that you could stick with during the years?

NICK: No. If I had, I might be afraid I'd miss it when time to retire came along.

PROFESSORS: What do you think of Shakespeare?

NICK: I'll give you a one-liner: I consider him a theatrical man whose writing was changed.

PROFESSORS: Could you give us laymen some gambling advice?

NICK: I don't believe any of you really need it. However, the best way to play is to always set a limit for yourself. Stick to it. If you're taking a beating, don't try to get even and lose twice as much. Slow down. If you're winning, keep betting more. Push.

PROFESSORS: Do you advise people against gambling?

NICK: Never. I show them reasons not to gamble. In this land of freedom you can't forbid or tell an American not to do something. He'll go out and do it just to spite you. It's the democratic way of life. Prohibition was an example. Did it stop anyone from drinking?

PROFESSORS: If you are knowledgeable, can you generally win at gambling?

NICK: With friends who are not as smart, yes. In a gambling house, no, if you play any length of time. After four or five hours that little devil, percentage, small as it seems, teaches you a lesson. Of course, any player can hit a hot spell and quit. That's different. Then you can beat the house.

PROFESSORS: In what form of gambling are the odds greatest against you?

NICK: Slot machines. All you get in the long run is exercise.

PROFESSORS: What was the most tremendous run of luck you ever saw?

NICK: I could cite myself several times when I made eighteen or twenty passes. However, the finest streak I ever heard of was executed by a Mrs. Alex Troffey, an eighteen-year-old girl. At Reno she played the ten-cent slots for an entire day and night until noon of the next day, and without hitting a jackpot finished eight dollars and ninety cents ahead.

PROFESSORS: If you win, say two hundred thousand, or lose two hundred thousand, is there a difference in the way you feel inside?

NICK: Absolutely no difference. I'll control my mind. Block it out with philosophy.

PROFESSORS: Do you have any advice to give someone who is going to gamble, besides having a set limit?

NICK: Use self-control. Don't be gripped in a rising fever. If the fever gets you, you'd sell your own mother for a few chips. Go to the washroom and splash cold water on your face. Reason with yourself. Someone has to lose. Why shouldn't it be you?

PROFESSORS: Have your gambling losses been higher than anyone's in the world?

NICK: Far from it. Phillip Armour, the packing house magnate, in three days lost two hundred million dollars trying to corner wheat in the Chicago Board of Trade.

PROFESSORS: If you have any repressions, how do you rid yourself of them?

NICK: By going to the gym and punching a bag. A shooting gallery would do the same for me except that I hate excessive noise.

PROFESSORS: Who was the most reckless gambler you ever knew?

NICK: Mike Todd. He was a plunger who tried to pile up a big win in a short time.

PROFESSORS: Name an ultraconservative gambler you have known who was a rich man.

NICK: Louis B. Mayer. He never bet more than ten dollars on any of the horses he owned.

PROFESSORS: What happens when a gambler gets a rubber check?

NICK: A smart gambler won't take a check. A check means that the income tax people can get the scent of it. There's hardly anything a gambler can do about a bogus check but charge it off as a loss and resolve to be more discriminating the next time.

PROFESSORS: Which is the best way to cut cards to safeguard yourself?

NICK: Pull a packet of them from the center of the deck. Put these atop the deck. Repeat four or five times. When finished, square up the cards and cut a few times the regular way.

PROFESSORS: Which gamblers have you most admired?

NICK: Richard Canfield the most. Also "Diamond Jim" Brady. He was a high roller. I'd wager he lost at least five pounds through perspiration every dice game. The man was so huge, he bought two seats to the Ziegfield Follies just to be comfortable. What I admired most about him was that he gave a fortune to found the Urological Institute at Johns Hopkins Hospital, Baltimore.

PROFESSORS: Is roulette a better game for men or women?

NICK: Women. A man can get dizzy watching the little white ball spin around, but it would have no effect on some women, who are in that condition to start with.

PROFESSORS: Do you have anything in common with racketeers?

NICK: Only that we deal in the same commodity: cash.

PROFESSORS: Are you a believer in hunches?

NICK: No. Decidedly not. I'd sooner play against one than on one.

PROFESSORS: Are you an atheist or agnostic?

NICK: No. I am a believer in God, but not of immortality of the soul. Infrequently I go to church, which I consider more or less hypocrisy. You can pray just as effectively at home. Religion to me is portable, to be carried around inside of you.

PROFESSORS: What nationality has the best gamblers?

NICK: I can't answer that. I've played against fine Anglo-Saxon gamblers and standouts that are Jews, Greeks (not including myself), Italians, Irish, and Orientals. I think that Jewish gamblers are more prolific. Some bookmakers have ninety-eight percent Jewish customers. The Jewish nervous systems seem to require more action than the Christian.

PROFESSORS: Which would you choose first for an enjoyable evening, a beautiful girl or a poker game?

NICK: A poker game.

PROFESSORS: Do you feel that being a professional gambler has been a social stigma?

NICK: Quite the contrary. It has meant an open sesame to all doors. Only with a few amateur athletes have my relations been injured. Any association between them and me may lead to rumors of a fix.

PROFESSORS: Do you lose your temper often?

NICK: I can't afford to in gambling. If emotions creep into your play, the results could prove fatal. The few temper tantrums I've experienced were sparked by dishonesty or stupidity. Stupidity irks me. Oscar Wilde once said, "There is no sin but stupidity." I agree with him.

PROFESSORS: You mentioned percentages. Do they affect all players the same?

NICK: No. An expert is a man who knows how to lose less than the average player. He can, by his proficiency, reduce the percentages against him.

PROFESSORS: Has anybody you've beaten for a huge amount of money ever committed suicide over the loss?

NICK: No. My conscience is clear on that. I never play with people who cannot afford to lose. I never caused self-destruction in anyone.

After the death of his parents, during his lean as well as his lush years, Nick never neglected his sister, Maria. She was living in Thessaloniki, Greece, and according to Jim Harakis, a friend of long standing (rumored a distant cousin) who once worked for the U. S. State Department, Nick sent her vast sums of money throughout the years.

Maria was destined to outlive her illustrious brother by a few years.

Regretfully, Nick allowed an optimistic broker to talk him into investing in the cotton market. It was virtually the only business deal he ever engaged in where it was necessary to affix his signature to any documents. He was almost fearful he might show a profit in this speculation and it would be declarable for income tax, although the tax bite had no sharp teeth in those days. Despite the fact that Nick won, and claimed he lost, five hundred million dollars in a lifetime, he paid no income tax. Nevertheless, he filled out tax forms, declaring his business to be that of "speculator."

The 1929 stock market crash erased his fears of being obliged to pay Uncle Sam a tax on his business profits. He lost $750,000.

Despite the fact that he often denounced roulette because of the high odds, he battled the wheel a number of times in international gaming spots. Twice during the 1930s he invaded Monte Carlo, once breaking one of the banks. His luck was not as good at the Cannes casino, where he was said to have dropped $120,000 to an opposing group that included a cousin of King Alfonso XIII of Spain.

With the opening of the Santa Anita racetrack in Arcadia,

California, in the mid-thirties, Nick was a daily visitor and
could always be located in the same box, along with his guests.
A steady stream of humanity approached him for touches and
tips. He was equally generous with both, but only a single
example of the latter clung to his memory.

It involved a friend, Hy Goldbaum. Goldbaum looked
glum and Nick asked him if anything was wrong.

"Plenty," Goldbaum answered. "I haven't cashed a bet in a
month and I'm in debt up to my ears." As he happened to be a
rather tall fellow, his height spoke for his money troubles.

Nick was in a benevolent mood. He sympathized with
Goldbaum. No man could have such a professional mourner's
expression and not have his worries.

"If that's the case, Hy," he said, "I'm going to give you one
in the third." He whispered a name into Goldbaum's ear.

Goldbaum's face became even sadder. "I appreciate the tip,
Nick, only I don't have much betting money."

"Well, you do now," Nick returned, handing him $100.

The horse won, paying $33.

Goldbaum practically did a dance of joy, his face glowing
neon, as he paid Nick back the loan and showed him a thick
roll of bills. "I've got enough to pay off all my debts and
some left for a couple of bets." He peeled off $600, removed
one of his shoes, and stored the money inside. "This goes for
the back rent and it never comes out," he said emphatically.

Nick saw him again after the sixth race. Goldbaum didn't
appear too happy. "I lost a little," he admitted, "but I'm all
right and the rent is still here, safe and sound." He tapped his
shoe significantly.

Just before post time for the last race of the day, Goldbaum
spied Nick going into the paddock with one of the trainers,
then coming out alone. He sensed he was on to something.
"Give me one," he gasped, rushing up to him.

"Number three," Nick advised.

Goldbaum had only a few seconds to spare. He sprinted to

the window. "Six hundred dollars on Number Three," he screamed at the teller, lifting his foot high and putting it on the counter.

The teller glanced distastefully at Goldbaum's foot, asking, "Where's your money, sir?"

"It's right here in the shoe," cried Goldbaum, unlacing his footwear and dumping the money out.

He managed to place his bet in time, and the horse won, paying $10.80.

There was an actor called Thousand Faces who came into Louis B. Mayer's box after each race and showed a winning ticket. He seemed to be trying to impress the movie mogul in order to wangle a part in a picture. It was beyond the realm of reality that a man could be this lucky, or smart, whichever the case might be. Nick put a friend named Dick Reiner on his tail, and Reiner had an interesting report. Thousand Faces was betting on every horse; thus he was consistently able to produce winning tickets. Nick kept his secret.

Santa Anita was only one of the tracks to which he journeyed. Every August he followed society's trail leading to Saratoga Springs for a month of thoroughbred racing, gambling, and hot mineral baths. Here, in the early 1930s, America's millionaires arrived in private railroad cars, accompanied by one to two dozen servants who readied their mansions for entertainment. If they owned no house they rented one, the monthly tariff running as high as $15,000. Gourmet millionaires brought their own chefs.

The affluent horsey set with which Nick was on intimate terms included such prominent names as Herbert Bayard Swope, Plunket Stewart, the Lorillards, Pierre Sr. and Jr., Colonel E. R. Bradley, Marshall Field, F. Skiddy von Stade, Thomas Hitchcock, Albert Bostwick, Cornelius Vanderbilt, John Sanford, Samuel D. Riddle, William Woodward, and the John Hay Whitneys.

Nick was particularly fond of the Whitneys, and less than a

year before death claimed him, dined with Liz at La Rue's on the Sunset Strip of Los Angeles. In Saratoga Liz, an outdoors woman, rode horseback every morning, wearing a priceless emerald necklace with her riding habit. One afternoon, after an evening of nightclubbing and gambling with Nick and her husband, she astounded those sitting around her in the clubhouse boxes by attending the races in an evening dress.

At the races Nick often sat with Sunny Jim Fitzsimmons, known as the grand old man of the turf, an habitual August racing visitor. When this pair put their two heads together to decide on a winner, it would almost take an unusual turn of events to keep their selection out of the money.

Not only did the rich populate this lively upper New York State spa, but a medley of others followed in their wake, including bookies, pimps, touts, prostitutes, gangsters, con men and petty fast-buck operators. The local police were hard pressed to keep them under observation.

Although the early thirties saw America in the grip of the Great Depression, the purse strings of the Saratoga millionaires were not drawn tighter until a few years later. Then, even though the resort's restaurant prices plummeted, they still remained far above the reach of Mr. Average Citizen. At the height of the monied era, some Saratoga dinners cost $100.

Two of the Saratoga bookmakers—the place was a mecca for them—were made famous by Damon Runyon: The Dancer, who entertained his customers and drummed up business by the execution of fancy steps while wearing oversized suits; and Gloomy Gus, whose facial expression led you to believe he had just viewed some horrendous tragedy. A bet was once made that Gloomy Gus wouldn't smile all day. Taking literary license, Runyon legally plagiarized their slang and coloquialisms. Two of his most famous maxims were born in Saratoga: "Don't gamble" and "All horse players die broke." He himself violated the first one and proved the second to be wrong.

In Saratoga Nick stayed at the United States Hotel. He always went into the hotel the back way because the main entrance was crowded with track losers trying to make a loan. As he was once sneaking into the back door, a thin man blocked his way.

"My name is Jimmy Sargent," the man said. "I've been waiting to see you for three hours and I hope you can help me."

It was the same old story. Nick started to put his hand into his pocket, deciding to hand him $500.

"Don't get me wrong," the man said, "I'm no bum. I'm going to California on a cattle car in the morning, but I'm stone broke. Could you lend me half a buck so I can get some sandwiches on the way out to the Coast?"

Without cracking a smile, Nick gave him a dollar, saying, "Look, you may not like California and want to come back, so here's something to tide you over for the return trip."

The panhandler was grateful.

The casinos and nightclubs were owned and operated by a syndicate of tough guys, and on their ruling board of directors sat Dutch Schultz, Lucky Luciano, Owney Madden, and Waxey Gordon. They knew and admired Nick. Many whom they didn't admire were under water, their feet encased in a block of concrete. They had seen Nick, once in the Grand Union Hotel and twice in the United States Hotel—sprawling hostelries of excellence that were a block long—play $100,000 freeze-outs of single-handed stud.

Of the fearsome four, it was Dutch Schultz—*né* Arthur Flegenheimer—whom Nick knew best. Had he kept the name Flegenheimer, it wouldn't have frightened a fly off a wall, but the mere mention of Dutch Schultz could empty a street or send people diving under tables.

"That boy has a fine future," Nick speculated on Schultz, neglecting to add "in crime." He first met Schultz when the Dutchman worked for Jack "Legs" Diamond, who, in turn, ostensibly worked for Arnold Rothstein, but had much going for him on the side that fell into his own pocket.

The rise of Dutch Schultz was meteoric. He started serving an apprenticeship with the Diamond Brothers, Jack and Eddie, drove a bootlegging truck for Rothstein, and eventually controlled a two-million-dollar-weekly policy racket.

Nick met him when Schultz was a cocky kid selling beer in the Bronx in the afternoon and at night moving downtown to try commingling with the Broadway bigshots. After observing his youthful energies and push, Nick picked him as a "future power in the underworld."

They went to the movies together a few times, usually to gangster pictures. This type of show made Schultz nervous, and he commented to Nick, "I don't think they're true to life."

Nick asked, "Why?"

"Well," Schultz said, "the bad guys always get knocked off in the ending."

"That's to please the censors," Nick explained.

Schultz nodded. "Yeah, I suppose so. But it's not realistic."

Just how realistic the writing was he would discover in 1925.

Schultz hit Nick for a loan to expand his beer route, and Nick gladly gave him the money. The route increased rapidly, and within a year Schultz repaid the loan and tried to add on some interest, which Nick declined to accept. Schultz seemed eternally grateful.

When he opened up a classy establishment in Saratoga with his three partners and business started off slowly, he sought out Nick. "I need a promotional stunt," he said.

Nick waited.

"Would you, as a personal favor to me, 'front' the place?" he asked, and went on, ". . . only for two weeks to help me get going. You're sure to draw a crowd by just being there

. . . four hours each night. Nine until one o'clock." He paused for breath. "I'll give you twenty-five grand for the two weeks. What do you say, Nick?"

Nick shook his head. "I can't agree to those terms."

"Listen," Schultz said, "I'll throw in an extra five grand."

"My terms or nothing, Dutch."

Schultz asked what they were.

"I'll do it for free, or I won't do it."

The happy Dutchman threw his arms around him. "My God, Nick, there's no friend like you. This is the second big favor you've done for me," he recalled.

"Everything runs in threes," Nick said, not realizing his prophetic powers.

Although Nick agreed to help out Schultz, he realized he had broken one of his ironclad rules. In any connection with gambling he had vowed to himself to be a player and have no tie-ins with the management. "Just this once I'll do it," he told himself.

The presence of the Greek, sartorially resplendent in evening clothes, standing just inside the casino as a greeter, jammed the place. He kept up his end of the verbal agreement, and at its expiration—despite the pleadings of Schultz, who offered him a permanent job—he was a free man again.

Easy though the job had been, at its conclusion Nick said, "I felt like shackles had been removed from my body."

One morning in 1935 Nick was preparing for bed at the Alamac Hotel. The hour was 3:15 A.M. He was scheduled to catch the train for Chicago the next day and then go on to Los Angeles. He heard a knock on the door.

"Who is it?" he asked cautiously.

"Dutch. Dutch Schultz."

He recognized the voice and unlocked the door, admitting the gangster. Schultz came in carrying a large, tightly strapped, battered suitcase. Setting it down in the center of the floor, he flopped into a chair, lit a cigarette, and inhaled deeply. After he expelled the smoke he coughed slightly and reminded, "Remember when you said everything runs in threes?"

Nick remembered.

Schultz took another drag on the cigarette. "You've done me two big favors in my life. Could you do me one more?"

"Name it."

Schultz pointed to the suitcase. "That's it."

"It isn't big enough for a body," Nick joked.

Schultz said, "Just keep it for me. When I'm ready I'll come and get it from you."

"I'll take care of it," Nick agreed after a long moment of consideration. "Only one question. Why me?"

Schultz ground out his cigarette in the ashtray and started for the door. "Because you're the only completely honest man I know."

He left.

Nick stared at the suitcase, picked it up, and put it in the closet. The following day it accompanied his own meager luggage to Chicago for a week, then to Los Angeles. There it was stored in the baggage room of the Beverly Wilshire Hotel.

He completely forgot about it.

Then, some months later he picked up the *Los Angeles Times* to learn that Arthur Flegenheimer, known to the public as Dutch Schultz, was dead, riddled by bullets from the guns of a rival gang in a Newark tavern.

Poor Dutch, he thought, feeling saddened. Suddenly the suitcase came to mind. After much difficulty he located the baggage check for the piece of luggage and handed it to a bellboy with the instructions, "Bring up a hammer and a chisel."

The suitcase and the tools arrived. Far from an excellent lockpicker, Nick went to work. He smiled, thinking how some of his notorious acquaintances could have snapped the lock open in a matter of seconds. At length, after hitting his fingers once, he pried the lock off.

Opening the suitcase, he gasped.

It was filled with crisp U.S. currency, arranged in neat stacks of thousand dollar bills. He counted, and the total was a staggering $5,000,000. Schultz, he surmised, must have wanted it hidden for tax purposes, or from his partners.

The reason was of no importance. It was his money now—an unexpected windfall.

Las Vegas

NICK the Greek's protracted and faithful romance with the city of Las Vegas, Nevada, like so many love affairs that end compatibly, got off to a shaky start. It was both natural and inevitable that he would be drawn to this Western state that formerly depended on silver mining and the divorce trade to bolster its sagging economy.

In 1930 Las Vegas, the desert trading center of southern Nevada, had a population of 5,165 sunbaked citizens. A year later the state legislature passed a law legalizing gambling. The boom was slow to begin. At first it was a mirage. But in 1940 the farsighted saw the writing on the desert sands, and they spelled out BONANZA. From that year on the pace of development rivaled the speed of sound. Today this American Baghdad can boast of nearly 300,000 inhabitants, few of whom do not indulge in games of chance.

On his first trip Nick rode in a chauffeur-driven car owned by his friend Carl Laemmle, Sr., the founder of Universal Pictures. They traveled in virtual silence. The immensity of the desert surrounding them, with its flat tabletop of sand stretching to the horizon, filled Nick with depression and brooding. To some the monotony of the quiet, unbroken landscape would have meant inner peace and meditation. To Nick, who liked to live in a crowd, it represented sheer boredom. Nothing mildly stirred his interest except an occasional windpropelled tumbleweed rolling along the shoulder of the ribbon of concrete; it, at least, was a form of action.

He had heard much about Las Vegas. "Wide open," they told him, and those words conjured a pleasing picture guaranteed to quicken his pulsebeat.

When the car stopped along the main drag, Fremont Street, dust swirls were spiraling like miniature cyclones to spew their contents over the dirty wooden sidewalks.

Alighting, Nick and Laemmle found the town crowded with Eastern tourists in new Western clothes, railroaders, silver, gold, and oil prospectors, unbathed cowboys, and Indians wrapped in blankets.

The two clubs were jammed with draw poker players—cowpokes, sourdoughs, prospectors whose faces were hidden behind forests of whiskers, and expressionless Indians. Nick sat down in a vacant chair. He was unrecognized. Noting his impeccable attire, a grizzled prospector muttered, "Another dude."

There are certain people in the world who simply cannot feel relaxed and comfortable in a sport shirt, sloppy slacks, and loafers. They are uncomfortable in so-called comfortable clothes. They won't venture in public with even slightly mussed hair or a day's growth of beard. They suffer much loss of perspiration, but never of dignity. Nick was a charter member of this club.

The players looked at him askance.

He had not intended sitting in the game. But the appearance of the players, their Central Casting physiognomy, fascinated him; and most important of all, he could add, sans embellishments, this adventure to his already bulging repertoire.

The players looked easy. They didn't seem to measure up to the standards of high-action gamblers Nick had competed against. How wrong he was! Try as he might, he couldn't penetrate the wilderness of whiskers or the impassive visages of the Indians.

He dropped $21,000. The mishap brought no financial worries; he had much of the Dutch Schultz accidental endowment stored in Los Angeles safe deposit vaults. It was the humiliation. He swore Laemmle (who couldn't stop laughing) to secrecy. But they were a pair of playful kidders, and now it was the studio executive's turn to stick the needle into the thick-skinned Greek.

"So the greatest gambler in the world is taken by a bunch of desert drifters," Laemmle howled in mock derision. "The learned professor bows to the illiterates."

Nick grimaced.

"Quote me a line from one of your poets or philosophers to describe how you feel," Laemmle demanded.

Nick spoke up quickly. "No creature smarts so little as a fool," he said humbly.

"Who wrote that?" Laemmle asked.

"Alexander Pope," Nick answered, naming the English poet who died in 1744.

"Hmmmm," Laemmle mused, "that's pretty good. Send him over to Universal; we could use a new writer."

Nick studied his friend's face. "I just wonder if you aren't really serious, Carl."

The next day as they climbed into Laemmle's car and headed toward the Coast, Nick said pensively, "I left a little something in that town, and one of these days I'm coming back to get it."

"Maybe by that time some of the players will have shaved," Laemmle chuckled.

Every day Nick's reputation soared higher. He had grown full bloom into a living legend. He tried to underplay, to live down his exploits, but he couldn't. Everyone, it seemed, loved a gambler with temerity. Men and women, young and old, could easily identify with his exploits. People on the street who recognized him nudged others to whisper, "There's Nick the Greek!"

He began to bemoan the name. If he overheard anyone referring to him by what he called "the rude tense" (Nick the Greek), he would sharply rebuke them, even going so far as to stop strangers by grabbing their arms and stating, "My name is Nicholas Dandolos," and while holding them in an iron grip, slowly spelling "D-a-n-d-o-l-o-s."

One of his favorite hangouts was the Vine Street Brown Derby in Hollywood. In those days there were no plugs at the tables for telephones, so when Nick received one of his numerous lunchtime calls, a page boy would walk through the crowded room singing out, "Call for Nick the Greek! Call for Nick the Greek!"

Nick always corrected him, but the boy was forgetful.

Early in World War II a select corps of Greek mountain troops was fighting heroically—although they were woefully lacking in equipment—against the invading German divisions. Nick was reading an overseas dispatch in the *Los Angeles Examiner* that praised the courage of the Greeks. He swelled with pride. These were his people.

Just then the absentminded page boy—finally having learned his lesson—shouted, "Call for Mr. Dandolos!"

Nick signaled for him to come over to the table. "In the future," he instructed the bewildered youth, "you had better call me Nick the Greek."

Besides the Brown Derby, Nick often dined at Perino's, Dave Chasen's, or Mike Romanoff's. In the company of women he would nightclub at Herman Hover's famed Ciro's or the Mocambo, Sunset Strip niteries where the movie-star-autograph seekers gathered.

Although he did not relish memories of his initial trip to Las Vegas, there was something compelling about the little desert community that drew him back again and again from 1940 to

1943. Finally he decided to become a resident. In those years there were only three clubs in downtown Vegas and three hotels on "the Strip."

Growth became phenomenally rapid. From an olden-day watering hole for cowboys, Indians, stagecoaches, and prospectors, multimillion-dollar resort hotels mushroomed. Before long, four major highways would bring motorized tourists, plus seven airlines and the Santa Fe Railroad.

Nick watched the Queen City expand from a sandbox to a resort city welcoming ten million yearly visitors. In fact, he helped it attain size. Reluctantly he became a tourist attraction. The Chamber of Commerce might prefer to keep it under their Western hats, but there was a period when they received more tourist inquiries about Nick the Greek than they did about their enormous man-made water attraction, Boulder Dam.

Nick's chances for legitimate profit other than from gambling in the flourishing desert city were multifold. He turned them all down. Property along the Strip that now sells for nearly $1,000 per foot could once have been his for $35 an acre. Many who had low cash reserves and owed him gambling debts offered him property for settlement. He wanted no part of land. "Just enough," he said, "to stand on by a table." Property ownership meant inscribing the name Nicholas Andrea Dandolos on a deed. The very thought of it was appalling. Hotels worth millions begged him to accept generous percentages. Among these were the Sands, the Last Frontier, the Desert Inn, El Rancho Vegas, and the Flamingo.

For an interest in the above-mentioned places little was required of Nick: merely to run the gambling casinos or permit the hotels to use his name. This was actually a small enough request and certainly not taxing on him, yet he refused every offer, each proposition.

"There's an old saying among bookmakers," he pointed out. "It's 'You can't book 'em and bet 'em.' I would have had to abide by this if I owned a piece of one of the casinos. It would have robbed me of all betting thrills to stay out of the action. I couldn't have that. Better to play and to lose. The game is the thing."

Nick always said, "Under no circumstances go against the green cloth unless prepared to lose a limited amount." He was referring to the percentages. He called percentages "inhuman devils whose brains are a composite of unbeatable figures," and the house limit "a brake that brings you to a grinding halt before you can get even."

He could have allied himself with these "devils" and made a fortune. But he chose to fight them, knowing it would be a losing battle. "It was a hopeless struggle," he recalled, "the same as attacking an atomic weapon with a short-bladed knife or attempting to scale Mt. Everest without shoes. But the challenge was compelling. I couldn't resist it. I was well aware it was a fallacy of reason."

How long did he last battling the percentages?

"For eleven years I held my own. During this period I won ten million dollars and I lost about the same amount, and eventually what remained of the Dutch Schultz money. After a lifetime of gambling I stood, financially, about the same as I was when I went to Canada to seek my fortune."

There were times when Nick would talk the pit bosses into raising or entirely removing the house limits. When this occurred he often burned the casinos. Before long they got smart and imposed a limit on his bets.

His favorite hotels were the Last Frontier, the Thunderbird, and the Sands. He didn't pay a dime at any of them. The management was happy to give him a room or a suite gratis for as long as he cared to stay. Once the word got around that Nick the Greek was at such-and-such a hotel, tourists beat a path to its casino doors to stand four deep around any table at which he was gambling. He also gambled privately with any high rollers who came to town.

Las Vegas is not shorthanded when it comes to beautiful women. They are omnipresent, represented by divorcées, tourists, waitresses, chorines, and prostitutes. Nick had his pick of the field. It was customary for him to dine with a girl or girls and walk into the casinos with one on each arm. Beautiful showgirls became his trademark. But they were only window dressing. None in Las Vegas could wrench him away from his true love—gambling.

He was fond of leisurely dinner with a woman—a dinner of many courses served with the proper wines. He was a talker at dinner. He had a captive audience, and he would fill her ears with poetry, philosophy, compliments. Should he notice his date struggling to cut a steak, he would do it for her.

Here is what a bosomy girl in the chorus line had to say about him:

"I'd prefer to date Nick before any man I know. He's exciting, educated, entertaining, and considerate. I once spilled some red wine on my dress and he bought me a new one. No man is more generous. I feel physically safe with him. I'm not trying to belittle his sexual powers, which are above average. You simply know he isn't going to try to unzip anything or wrestle with you. His attitude is Old World. I guess you could call it courtly. Being of normal desires, he would naturally ask you to go to bed with him. After all, when he isn't gambling he's a human, you can be sure. Why, when this man asks you to bed, it's like receiving a gold-engraved invitation to a command performance. And what girl could refuse?"

Nick always carefully avoided eating in any greasy-spoon-type restaurant. He was extremely sensitive about unclean surroundings, poor service, and badly prepared food. He preferred a quiet, expensive place with subdued decor. "I can stand a hamburger," he confessed, "mainly because a variety of condiments can be added to disguise the taste, but a poorly cooked entrée is offensive to the taste buds, besides presenting a challenge to the digestive system."

Dancing was one of his favorite pastimes. He had a sweeping style, a combination of waltz and fox trot that commanded the attention of onlookers. It was pleasing, eye-catching, and graceful. He would whirl his partner at every opportunity.

In 1943 he developed a close friendship with actress Ava Gardner, a guest at El Rancho Vegas. One moonlit evening he took her to see the show at the Last Frontier. At its conclusion they went to the hotel lounge for dinner. Knowing that there would be dancing, and that he had put on new shoes that were too tight, he excused himself, went to his room, and changed them.

They ordered dinner. Ava scribbled on a piece of paper, "Please play a tango. Ava," and called a waiter, who took it to the orchestra. Both she and Nick had a fondness for tangos.

The orchestra leader complied with her request. As they walked to the dance floor, a few patrons started to snicker. Just before Nick's arm slipped around the actress' waist, the headwaiter tapped him on the shoulder.

"Pardon me, sir," he said politely. "It's none of my business, but you are wearing a black and white shoe."

Both Nick and his partner looked down at his feet. The headwaiter was right. In his haste Nick had put on two different color shoes.

"Pay no attention," Ava counseled. "Let's dance."

As the pair tangoed, other couples left the floor to watch, until they were the only dancers remaining. The gambler and the actress were spectacular.

Three days later Ed Sullivan wrote in his column:

Nick Dandolos, after losing a few million dollars in Las Vegas, to change his luck wore a black and white shoe, and in company with Ava Gardner broke three clubs.

The aftermath was that for the entire week tourist-gamblers were observed wearing different shoe combinations in Las Vegas and at racetracks around the nation.

"It is of such stuff that superstitions are commonly made," Nick contended, adding, "superstition is inherent in man's nature and is the poetry of life."

He never quite forgot what Dutch Schultz said to him in Saratoga: "Every gambling house in America should give you one percent of the profits and you should make thousands per day for as long as you live, for what you have done for legitimate gambling."

His answer to Schultz was, "A guaranteed income is a guaranteed bore."

On trips away from Las Vegas, Nick was the city's greatest booster. He was virtually a one-man chamber of commerce. His chief promotional pitches were: "Where else could you enjoy yourself for so little money?" and "Forget the old Vegas saying, 'It's a great place to visit, but don't bring your wife.' Bring her and she'll have the time of her life."

Yet if Nick read Las Vegas publicity in magazine articles or books where the writer, without permission, used his name, he raved and ranted, and threatened libel suits involving enormous sums of money, which he had no intention of instigating. A libel suit was the last thing he desired, with his name and photo in the newspapers!

He was incensed one year by a Las Vegas travel article that appeared in *Argosy Magazine*. It said:

There's no law that says you can't win, if you do play. Some of the professional gamblers, like Nick the Greek, as well as thousands of lucky amateurs, have come away with sizable stakes.

Nick claimed that a conservative man might read that, leave for Las Vegas, and ruin his life.

Completely overlooked by Nick were such pleasurable offerings of the desert city as golf, tennis, pool swimming, and lake fishing. A lover of spectator sports, he was never a participant in any of the aforementioned. His regard for them was low, his remarks about them acerbic:

Golf: Much ado about nothing. . . . Where the potbellied
ride in motor-driven carts and think of themselves as athletes.

Swimming: People should concentrate more on learning to
walk gracefully and leave swimming to the fish.

Tennis: This sport at least disproves the old motto, 'meek as
a lamb,' for the best tennis racket strings are from the guts
of that animal.

Fishing: A contest between the equipment manufacturers and
the unsuspecting.

Nick claimed he had neither an indoor nor an outdoor complexion. "My skin has absorbed its coloring from night lights
and green felt," he said. Always a lover of the indoors, he considered the outdoors only a transient place through which he
had to pass to get indoors again. Any stadium or racetrack
with a roof overhead he considered part of the indoors.

In his lone skirmish with the outdoors he was badly bested.
After a number of all-night gambling sessions in New York
City, he had a crazy idea: He needed rest and relaxation deep
in the bosom of nature. He departed for an Adirondack
mountain resort called Schroon Lake Village, where he registered as a guest at The Leland House, a large hotel overlooking
the nine-mile-long lake.

His first day he strolled in the woods wearing a coat, necktie, and spats. From a distance he watched a family of skunks,
and from closer range, a hedgehog, a porcupine, and numerous chipmunks. He gave a start of joy when he thought he
heard the rattling of dice. To his extreme disappointment, it
turned out to be a woodpecker carving a new home.

The second day he bought much fishing tackle, including a
rod and reel. From an enterprising local bait seller and high
school youth named M. Leo Friedman he purchased a can of
worms; then he hired the boy to row him in a rented boat. He
caught nothing.

In recalling the afternoon many years later, Friedman, now a lawyer and one of the town's leading businessmen, said, "He seemed unreal sitting in the stern of a rowboat. Part of the time he just looked up at the sky and recited poetry. Whether or not he caught a fish didn't seem to matter. A wind came up and the lake got very rough. There were whitecaps and the wind pitched the boat about rather dangerously. When we finally docked I asked him if he could swim, and he said, 'No.'"

The third day Nick just sat on the porch and rocked.

On the fourth day he consulted the one local physician, a Dr. Breen. "Doctor," he began, "I'm in very bad condition."

The doctor reached for his pulse and took an educated guess. "Can't sleep, eh, is that the trouble?" A number of his patients were nervous city people, and one glance at Nick's clothes placed him in this category.

"No," Nick told the doctor, "I sleep fine, the minute my head hits the pillow. That's the trouble."

Dr. Breen's hand fell away from Nick's pulse. This man needed a psychiatrist, he thought. Before he could offer any suggestions, Nick explained, "I've never been able to sleep before four or five in the morning in the city. Now I can't stay awake after nine P.M.

"Is that bad?" the puzzled doctor asked.

"It's very bad."

Dr. Breen suggested, "Maybe you ought to go back to the city."

"That's sound advice," Nick said, thanking him. "I'll take it."

He left immediately for New York, where the action was.

One night as Nick was leaving the Horse Shoe Club he was accosted by a Los Angeles minister. He was rather shocked to see the man, whom he knew fairly well, in Las Vegas. The minister hastily explained that he was gathering material for one of his forthcoming Sunday sermons.

"On the evils of gambling?" Nick guessed.

The minister acknowledged that would be the subject from the pulpit and said he was in town to witness it firsthand. Nick invited him to his room at the Sands for a chat. He wasn't sleepy, and even if he had been, the thought of intelligent conversation would have dispelled any wish to go to bed.

When they were comfortably seated, Nick mentioned that perhaps he could be of help by recalling some quotations from the past on the subject. The minister told him to go ahead, while he opened a notebook and waited with pen poised.

Nick spoke slowly so the minister could keep pace:

" 'By gambling, we lose both our time and treasure, two main things most precious to the life of man.'

" 'It is possible that a wise and good man may be prevailed on to gamble; but it is impossible that a professed gamester should be a wise and good man.'

" 'Keep flax from fire and youth from gaming.' "

He paused and waited for the minister, who was scribbling furiously, to catch up with his philosophical quotations.

"Enough?" Nick questioned.

"Just a few more, please," the minister said, readying a fresh page.

"Okay, Reverend," Nick said, "here goes. 'Gambling is the child of avarice, the brother of iniquity, and the father of mischief.'

" 'Gambling houses are temples where the most sordid and turbulent passions contend.'

" 'Cursed is the wretch enslaved to such a vice, who ventures life and soul upon the dice.'

" 'Sports and gaming, whether pursued from a desire for gain or the love of pleasure, are as ruinous to the temper and disposition of the one addicted as they are to his fame and fortune.' "

Nick stopped. The minister put away his notebook and said, "I want to thank you, Mr. Dandolos. I can take the majority of these quotations directly from context and weave them into my sermon."

Nick said he was happy to help a messenger of the Lord.

The minister shook hands with the gambler and thanked him effusively. Before he left he asked rather timidly, "I wonder if I might pose a question, Mr. Dandolos?"

Nick gave his permission.

"Well, then," the minister began hesitatingly, "I was wondering how you could retain these pearls of wisdom in your memory throughout the years, and not have them curb your gambling appetite. Therefore I must assume that you don't believe in them?"

Nick smiled. "Oh, I believe in them all right."

"But if such be the case," the wearer of the cloth rebutted, "why have they had no noticeable effect on you?"

Nick answered quickly, "Because each of these philosophers forgot, in his efforts to point up the evils of gambling, the important contribution it can make to a human."

"And what may that be, Mr. Dandolos?"

"Thrills," Nick said. "Just plain thrills . . . the emotional effect, the tremors and the tingles that can provide a tremulous excitement. Yes, Mr. Minister, it's the thrill that counts with me. Nothing else matters."

One event in the legendary life of Nick that did not reach the public took place at the Beverly Hills Hotel in 1946. Two of Hollywood's biggest movie tycoons, Joe Schenck of Twentieth Century Fox and Louis B. Mayer of Metro-Goldwyn-Mayer were arguing violently over which of the two giant studios would sign a voluptuous blonde. The blonde was Marilyn Monroe.

Each claimed her for his own studio. Overtures had been made. Now it was strictly up to Miss Monroe, but as yet she was undecided where to cast her lot. Schenck and Mayer were shrewd manipulators, masterful salesmen—operators who ferreted out angles that gave them an advantage in contractual matters. When they bucked heads—which they did now, both foreseeing a future fortune in the face and figure of this blonde Venus—it was like the impact of an irresistible force meeting an immovable object. The crash could be heard for miles.

For twenty minutes they shouted at each other, and Mayer, blustering, bullying and profaning, was outpointing his adversary in the invective department. Finally they both stopped yelling.

Schenck remarked, "L. B., this is not only bad for our hearts, it's getting us nowhere."

Mayer agreed. Craftily, he offered a proposition in which he had the edge. "Let's play a thousand-point game of two-handed pinochle for her contract." Mayer was considered a pinochle expert.

Schenck, after a moment of deliberation, agreed. Mayer could hardly conceal his exuberance. The contest was scheduled for the following evening in the hotel, and a time was set. Only the two of them were to be present.

"Better take some lessons tomorrow afternoon, Joe," Mayer's voice boomed.

Schenck didn't reply. He was too busy thinking.

The next night they sat down to play for the important contract. Mayer, running true to his usual form, took a 350-to-70-point lead after two deals.

He was about to shuffle the cards when Schenck raised the palm of his hand in a halting gesture. "Wait a second, L. B."

"What's the matter?" Mayer asked.

Schenck dabbed at his forehead with a handkerchief and then rubbed his stomach. "I don't feel so good," he said.

Mayer glanced at the score pad and snorted, "I wouldn't feel good either if I were down two hundred eighty points."

Resting his head in his hands, Schenck gasped, "A deal's a deal, L. B.; I'm not trying to welch. But I can't go on. I'm sick." He began coughing violently. When the spasm ended, he cleared his throat with difficulty and said, "I'll tell you what I'll do because I've given you my word on this."

"Just what will that be?" Mayer demanded impatiently.

The stricken film executive pushed back his chair and rose unsteadily to his feet. "I'm going home to bed. I can't play any more. But in the lobby I'll find someone I know and I'll send him up to finish the game. Is this satisfactory?"

Mayer voiced that it was perfectly satisfactory, and that for all he cared, Joe could send up anybody—from the Governor of California to a bellhop. Schenck left, clutching the pit of his stomach, muttering, "I must have been poisoned."

Mayer picked up the score pad, silently gloating. Ten minutes later in response to a gentle knock on the door, he called, "Come in!"

Nick the Greek entered the room.

"Good evening, L. B.," he said amiably.

The veins in Mayer's neck began to swell. "You, of all people!" he sputtered angrily.

Nick sat down and explained, "I saw Joe in the lobby and he . . ."

"Never mind," Mayer retorted. "It's my deal and the score's on the pad. I'm sure you know it's a thousand-point game."

He offered the cards for a cut. Nick cut six or seven times and pushed the deck toward his opponent.

"Deal," he said.

The outcome was that Mayer and his studio bowed out of the transaction. Miss Monroe signed the contract. The following day Schenck met Nick and, after thanking him for beating Mayer, handed him an envelope.

It contained five thousand dollar bills.

"For the work you did for Fox Studios, for your countryman Spyros Skouras, for Darryl Zanuck, and for me, we are grateful," Schenck said.

Nick handed back the money. "I couldn't accept it, Joe," he said politely. "It wasn't work. I enjoyed it."

It wasn't long before Miss Monroe began coining money for Fox Studios. And it wasn't long before an irate Louis B. Mayer realized he had been taken—that a canny Joe Schenck had tricked him by planting Nick the Greek in the lobby.

Nothing that ever cropped up was considered important enough to halt Nick's gambling once he entered a game. Two severe physical setbacks failed to put him out of action.

The first occurred at the Las Vegas Club in the downtown section of the city where Nick was playing faro bank. Deciding to go to the gentleman's room—despite the fact that he always preached against allowing the call of nature to interfere with gambling—he slipped on a tiled floor and broke an arm.

"I give advice by the bucket, but take it by the grain," an angry Nick chided himself in front of singer Gene Austin, who assisted him into a cab bound for a doctor. The arm was found to be broken and was set and placed in a sling. The doctor's advice was "Go home and rest."

Instead, Nick returned to the Las Vegas Club and resumed play. Austin saw him come in and commiserated with him and asked how he felt.

"It could have been a lot worse," Nick answered. "Why, it could have happened to somebody I liked."

The second deterrent to his gambling was closer to being catastrophic. In the Thunderbird Hotel where he was residing, Nick slipped a colored sock over an ankle scratch and headed for the crap table. After three hours his leg began to swell. In the lavatory he rolled up his trouser leg for an inspection. His limb had become purple.

One of the pit bosses saw the discoloration. "You better go get that attended to," the casino employee advised.

Nick stubbornly refused. "The action's too fast to miss right now," he said.

Alarmed by what he had seen, the pit boss called the house physician. By the time the doctor arrived, Nick was in considerable pain, but he refused to leave the table. The doctor, familiar with his tenacity, stooped under the table to conduct an examination. Finished, he straightened up.

Nick had just bet the house limit against the shooter. "What's the verdict?" he asked.

"You're going to the hospital," the doctor ordered.

The shooter crapped out, and the pile of hundred dollar chips in front of Nick grew to miniature mountain size. He was having a wonderful time. He turned to face the doctor.

"I'm not leaving," he declared flatly. "What can you do for me?"

The doctor said he could try penicillin. Nick told him to go ahead. The doctor groped in his bag, filled a hypodermic with the miracle drug, squatted under the table, and shot the antibiotic into him.

"The next time I come here to see you, you'll be dead," the doctor gravely predicted.

"When will that be?"

"In two hours."

"I'll be waiting," Nick said as he placed another bet.

Two hours later the doctor appeared again. The leg swelling had subsided considerably.

Nick said, "I've won sixty-two thousand dollars since you were last here, Doctor. Not bad for a dead man."

The doctor sighed heavily and walked away.

Only once did Nick ever consider hiring a secretary—a thought that was readily dismissed. In 1954, following a series of three articles in the now defunct *Collier's Magazine* titled "Nick the Greek: King of the Gamblers," by Richard Donovan, a writer collaborating with Hank Greenspun, owner of the Las Vegas Sun, mail from readers began flooding the post office marked merely "Nick the Greek, Las Vegas, Nevada."

Every letter asked for money. There was a general sameness about them, with the exception of one that was so ridiculous it appealed to his sense of humor. It read:

Dear Mr. Dandolos:
I know that you are a humanitarian, and for that reason will be interested in my invention. It is an invisible ray powerful enough to paralyze the entire population of a nation, thus preventing war. I'll need $100,000 to finance the finishing touches on the ray and make it workable.
Think of what this insignificant amount of money will do for mankind. You would be the patron and sponsor of WORLD PEACE!
For a guaranteed safe future,
                                        (signed) ———

Nick dictated the following letter to the public stenographer at the Sands Hotel, instructing her to sign his name to it on the typewriter:

Dear Mr. ———
Any contribution to peace in the world is most worthy, and I am all for it. $100,000 is a mere pittance if your invisible ray is operative. However, I do not relish buying a pig in a poke. Please send me a photograph of your paralyzing ray, even though incompleted.
                                        Sincerely,
                                        Nicholas Dandolos

By return mail he received an answer:

Dear Mr. Dandolos:
Thanks for your prompt reply.
I only wish it were possible for me to photograph my wonderful

invention, but alas, such is impossible. I can understand why this
is not conceivable to you, for you are a man of letters and not
science. Therefore I will explain.

The ray itself, being invisible, is incapable of being seen. Therefore
it would not be perceptible to your vision. I am afraid if I sent a
photo of the machine that discharges the ray, it might fall into the
hands of spies and be duplicated. I hope you will agree that it
would be impossible to honor your request.

I await your contribution and your trust,

(signed) ———

Believing it time to end the farce, Nick dictated his final
letter:

Dear Mr. ———

I am afraid I cannot pay for something invisible. When, and if,
your invention is completed and will do what you claim, please
give me a firsthand demonstration against my worst enemy.

Cordially,
Nicholas Dandolos

He was to receive one more letter, a last appeal from the
inventor:

Dear Mr. Dandolos:

I have devised a way whereby your initial investment of $100,000
will be easily returnable and with a profit. Upon completion of
the paralyzing ray, before I turn it over to our government, I will
come to Las Vegas and perform this service for you:

I will paralyze everyone in the gambling casino, but you, each time
you roll the dice. Then, when everybody is immobilized, you can
turn over the dice to any point you wish, and then I'll bring people
back to life again.

How can you lose?

(signed) ———

Newspaper columnists have a fertile field in Las Vegas, one
of the easiest towns in which to pick up newsworthy items.
Every visiting journalist was drawn to Nick. He tried in his

gentlemanly way to discourage them, to turn away from their pleadings, to never allow them to stir him by irritation into controversy. He succeeded in doing this to a high degree. At the conclusion of an interview he still remained an enigma.

For example, this column by nationally syndicated newsman Jimmy Cannon contained the usual conjecture about the King of Gamblers. It was called "The Last of a Perishing Breed."

This was the clockless hour of the losers in Las Vegas. It was acey-deucey time when the desert wind blows the sand of the gambler's night, like mean confetti tormenting the slow-coming morning. The shooters were rolling to get out. The dealer's shift was the dead night's graveyard watch.

At a table in the coffee shop of the Stardust Hotel, patient with a murmurous chivalry, Nick the Greek waited for the players to arrive for the big poker game. He smoked a cigar with an old man's serenity, a gambler of mysterious solitude and gallant legend, the most famous of his kind, the most graceful of losers, the last of a perished species, the final survivor of his unremembered breed.

He is a player, and he bets into all the dealers' games. Never once, holding a million stashed in a satchel or flat pocket, has the Greek ever bought a piece of a dealer's hand. He comes to challenge the house in the licensed casinos now, just as he went up against Arnold Rothstein in the lofts above garages and in the hotel suites of the bootleg age.

Gambling has never been a business with him but a prolonged ecstasy. He plays as a monk must pray. He has bet fins on punks hustling one ball in hick poolrooms, and blown a million at least a dozen times.

No one knows where it came from. He is a loner, and he cherishes his aloofness, a hermit who lives in crowds. He has always worked a single hand and, ever since the beginning, they have wondered who stakes him. They're still guessing. No one counts his money. I've heard guys claim the King of Greece bankrolled him and also Dutch Schultz, the bootleg hoodlum, a syndicate of old country Greeks, a shoe manufacturer, and the owner of a movie studio.

At acey-deucey time, in the casino without a clock, Nick the Greek walked toward the poker table and bought a hand. Outside the desert wind disturbed the sand. The Greek drew two cards and bumped the raise. At the crap table the dealer told the shooter he was coming out for nine.

In his passionate worship of Las Vegas, Nick was a starry-eyed boy. To him the city was a mill of perpetual motion, grinding out merriment twenty-four hours a day. The place was a national hope chest, but never a fool's paradise. It was a little slice of heaven where the sun always shone and the air conditioning never failed.

His eyes were blinded to any existent evils. He saw only what he wanted to see. He studiously avoided discussions on anything concerning the city that was not Utopian, as exemplified by the ambiguity in these answers to an inquiring newspaper reporter:

REPORTER: Do you think any skimming [money hidden from tax collectors] goes on in the counting rooms?
NICK: I am unfamiliar with the term "skimming."
REPORTER: Aren't there a lot of unsavory characters with police records operating the hotels and clubs and running some of the games here?
NICK: [He quoted from James Joyce's *Ulysses*] "A man of genius makes no mistakes. His errors are volitional and are the portals of discovery." [And then he ad libbed] Besides, who of us are pure geniuses?

In his book *Las Vegas: City Without Clocks*, published in 1961, Ed Reid, who later co-authored the bestselling *Green Felt Jungle*, wrote about Nick:

The gambling frontier that came into existence when a money-desperate Nevada decreed itself exempt from the Federal law which might have throttled its chance for gaming wealth, found itself a hero in one Nicholas Andrea Dandolos.

He is the most fabulous gambler in the world to everybody except the men who run the casinos in Las Vegas. He is the symbol of dice and cards and the long green table to tourists, who stare at him goggle-eyed and kibitz whenever he is playing, but to the men who make their living from these tourists, he is something less than a curiosity. The fact is that they resent Nick the Greek; they resent the fact that in a world where gambling has created mostly one-track minds, where one's whole life is wrapped in the commercialism that evolves around picking up and laying down silver dollars, Nick the Greek is different. He is, in fact, the only famous gambler in the world. All others are mediocre compared to him.

Ecstatic over each new building excavation he saw, Nick watched the four-mile Las Vegas strip transformed from dirty grains of sand to a man-made Garden of Eden, green and fruitful both inside and outside the plush hotels. In 1966—the final year of his life—civic boosters pointed with pride to thirteen hotel-casinos, with four more in the process of being built.

According to the figures of a leading banker of the city, the gambling industry was providing 75 percent of the city's economy. In Clark County (where Las Vegas is situated) casino winnings totaled $187.5 million—$55.1 million from slot machines and $132.4 million from games and tables.

How much of this amount is contributed by men as opposed to women is incalculable, but it is correctly assumed that men are, by far, the heaviest dice-shooting and cardplaying gamblers, the women gravitating to keno, roulette, and the slots. Students of slot machines will tell you that few women quit play after hitting a jackpot and go home with the money. Deep in the throes of a rising fever, they feed the coins back into the maw of the iron monster.

A man was once overheard remarking that before he would

propose marriage to any woman he met in Las Vegas, he would first examine her hand for blisters. If he discovered some, he would know they were from pulling slot machine cranks—indicating that she was a foolish and compulsive gambler. He would back away from such a marital prospect.

Nick had often sounded warnings about underestimating sweet old ladies in gambling. "One minute they seem too helpless and befuddled to cash their welfare checks, and the next minute they strip the shirt off your back," he contended. He did not consider women exceptionally fine gamblers. "Where there is neither love nor hatred in the game, women's play is mediocre."

It did not seem just that the city that had compounded and titillated his pleasures for so many years could be the scene of a near Waterloo for the King of Gamblers, but that is exactly what happened poolside at the Thunderbird Hotel when he matched wits with wealthy hotel owner Ray Ryan in fifteen daily sessions of two-handed lowball. Nick lost $550,000.

It was a monetary defeat from which he never fully recovered, a giant blow that sent his fortunes reeling.

At the time there were no outcries or alibis from Nick, and gamblers called it "the last big-stakes game." Fifteen years later details of the game, claims and counterclaims, were revealed in a Los Angeles Federal Court. It was here that a Federal Court jury convicted Johnny Marshall and Charles Del Monico of attempting to extract $60,000 annually in protection money from Ryan.

Prosecutor of the case was Assistant U. S. Attorney Thomas Sheridan, who successfully prosecuted the income tax trial that resulted in mobster Mickey Cohen being sent to jail in 1961. He was also the prosecutor of the Frank Sinatra, Jr., kidnap trial.

A third defendant in the Ryan case, Allen Smiley of Beverly Hills, was acquitted of any part in the conspiracy scheme.

Nick was a witness in the trial, claiming that the three men were simply trying to help him collect his losses from Ryan. "Ryan beat me out of the $550,000, and all the gamblers knew it," he claimed.

Arthur Crowley, Smiley's attorney, said in his opening statement, "Evidence will show that Ray Ryan cheated Mr. Nick Dandolos in a poker game, using a shortwave radio gimmick, and that none of these defendants extorted or threatened to get any money out of him."

(A similar gimmick later became famous after it was woven into the plot of *Goldfinger* by famed mystery writer Ian Fleming, published in 1959.)

Nick was not indicted in the case. Attorney Sheridan described him as an "unindicted conspirator."

Jim Harakas, a lawyer who formerly served with the Interior Department on a slum clearance program, with the State Department on a mission to Africa, and with the U. N. Relief and Rehabilitation Administration, acted as the payoff man for Nick. Back in Chicago, Nick had taken a liking to young Harakas and sent him to law school.

He said Dandolos accused Ryan of cheating him of $550,000, but demanded only $195,000 back. Harakas testified Ryan offered to pay $135,000 because it would embarrass him if anyone found out about it.

Nick said that he learned later that the card game was crooked. "A man came up to me and offered me ten thousand dollars," he said. " 'Nick,' he told me, 'Ray Ryan paid me twenty thousand dollars to cheat you.' "

Ryan testified at one point in the trial that Johnny Marshall told him that not even knowing Attorney General Robert Kennedy as a friend could save him if he did not comply with the demand for $60,000 protection money.

The threat was made, Ryan claimed, on May 1, 1963, in the Desert Inn Hotel, Las Vegas.

This 1949 debacle heralded the beginning of the dollar drain on Nick's bankroll. Gradually his money began to evaporate, and with it a slow deterioration in his health took place. When he played Ryan he was sixty-seven years old. Five years later he suffered the first of a series of heart attacks. Then after two years he was hospitalized at the Cedars of Lebanon Hospital, Los Angeles, for a hernia operation. His blood tended to demonstrate poor clotting tendencies. He also developed a kidney shutdown.

Nick became apprehensive. For the first time in his life he thought of dying. He also thought of his credit rating and his remarkable record of never having failed to meet a marker. And he remembered that he owed a few debts.

"I wanted to die without leaving any creditors," he said.

He instructed the nurse to telephone a trusted friend, Harry Goldenberg, a representative of the Sands Hotel with an office in Beverly Hills. Goldenberg came immediately to the hospital. Nick's voice was weak, and Goldenberg bent low over him to hear his words.

"Harry, I want you to do me a favor," he began, and his breathing was heavy and uneven. He mentioned the names of some men to whom he owed money and the specific amounts. They totaled $70,000. "If I die," Nick said, "I want you to pay off these gentlemen and give them my blessing." Beckoning his friend to come closer, he whispered into his ear where the money was hidden.

As it turned out, Nick recovered, and the first thing he did was to pay off his debts.

The second thing he did was to try to build up his bankroll by borrowing—something that in the past he had had no trouble doing.

It was different now. At seventy-four he was already beating the vital statistics averages. Friends were hesitant about lending him money. There could be a collection problem. Death could be hovering around the corner of the casino.

The Final Years

THE staggering lowball poker loss suffered by Nick at the Thunderbird Hotel triggered a series of gambling mishaps. Lady Luck completely deserted him. His star was on the wane. At his friend Benny Binion's Horse Shoe Club, deep in the heart of gambling row, downtown Las Vegas, the Greek plunged into a dice game as if money was going out of style.

"Up the limit," he requested, as he bought $20,000 worth of chips.

Binion nodded his okay. The table limit rose from $200 to $500, and $500 odds.

Word having reached the street that Nick was inside, the place was soon packed. They came to see the famed gambler, his face impassive, stooping slightly over the green table, battle the house. They were identifying with him. He was their gallant knight in shining armor. He had the guts, the stamina, the know-how to try to do what they couldn't.

True to custom, Nick played the back line. He played it to reduce the percentage against him by .01. He also played it for another reason. He claimed that once, and possibly twice, each evening one of the dice landed in a cocked position against the cushions, and should the throw favor the house, the stickman would quickly scoop up the dice. If the cocked dice favored the shooter, it was ruled not to count and had to be thrown again.

He played all night. He didn't always play in the conventional manner, but sometimes, as he did at the Horse Shoe Club, the way the pros call "by ear." In so doing, he wouldn't always watch the dice, but would rest his eyes. With a trained ear he followed the action, and tossed in or pulled back his chips automatically. It was impossible to tell by his face what his fortunes were. He might be losing two dollars or winning a hundred thousand, but it would never show.

By morning he had lost $200,000.

The loss was in markers . . . markers that would be locked in the club safe.

On a good night he lavishly tipped everybody working the table, sometimes up to $1,000. With bad luck he still tossed $200 or $300 in gratuities to the gentlemen with the sallow complexions.

He left for the Golden Nugget across the street, and discussed the table limit with owner Guy McAfee. McAfee wouldn't raise it. In two hours Nick was out another $60,000.

In markers.

He went from club to club, from hotel casino to hotel casino. Five days passed before a weary Nick crawled into bed. His losses had been tremendous; the exact sum for this unbroken period of play was never ascertained.

But all of it was in markers. These markers were his reputation. They had a time limitation.

Again fearful he would not awaken if he slept too many hours straight, he hired a woman to awaken him periodically by shaking his shoulder. Six hours later he was up and off for Reno and the Riverside Hotel casino, operated by two old friends from Detroit, Mert and Lou Wertheimer. Here he hit for about $25,000. From Reno he went to The Cal-Neva

Lodge, situated on the shores of magnificent Lake Tahoe, just across the California state line. The deep, scenic lake is too cold for comfortable swimming—which fits perfectly into the schemes of the gambling casino owners: instead of swimming, guests can always gamble, with a chance of getting into hotter water than the lake.

Nick stood for nine consecutive hours at the dice table, losing his Reno winnings and all the cash he had on him. His last $1,000 he took out of his hatband. He asked for chips on credit, the request a mere formality.

This time it was different.

Reports had drifted up from Las Vegas that Nick the Greek was tapped out. He was firmly refused credit. Nick was nonplussed. It seemed inconceivable that he, who had never welched on a personal debt or a marker, had suddenly been classified as a risk.

But a risk he had become.

He argued with the casino box men. He delivered a short, pithy speech: "You are stripping the clothes from a man cloaked with integrity. A physical injury could be much sooner forgotten than this insult. You are questioning my very honor."

The answer remained the same: "Sorry, Mr. Dandolos, no markers."

Angrily Nick left Lake Tahoe, vowing never to return. For the first time in his life his credit had been questioned.

It was much the same story upon his return to Vegas. The word had spread.

He left for Los Angeles, checking in at his old hotel, the Beverly Wilshire. A month later, after some wrangling with the manager, he checked out. It was presumed that he could not pay his bills. He moved to a smaller hotel, the Beverly Rodeo, and then to the Beverly Crest.

The years were racing along. He was growing old.

For action, he played at a suburb of Los Angeles, Gardena. Here, at the "poor man's Las Vegas," poker was legal and Nick was seen at the Monterey, Normandie, and Horseshoe Clubs. The games he sat in on had five and ten dollar limits. The house made a small cut from each individual player on the half hour.

He was asked, "Isn't this penny-ante poker a comedown for you?"

Certainly it was, but Nick was a proud man. "It's action, isn't it?" he answered defiantly, eyes glaring.

Periodically he flew to Las Vegas to battle again the odds up and down the Strip and on Fremont Stret. On these trips he carried a fresh bankroll. In the olden, golden days no one ever financed him. He had turned down all backers. Now he needed them. Desperately. He was glad to accept their money and engage in a partnership he did not relish, but he knew it was the only way he could still stay in the gambling scene.

The backers had percentage arrangements. Few profited.

At Santa Anita and Hollywood Park bettors were startled to see him at the two-dollar windows. Horse racing researchers, augmented by gamblers' and inside information, had dug up a handful of men who were said to have beat the races. They uncovered Pittsburgh Phil, Chicago O'Brien, Riley Granner, "Betcha Million" Gates, Arnold Rothstein, and the newcomer into this select gathering, Nick the Greek. The list was now shortened by one, Nick's name having been lopped off.

Nick had a chance in early 1953 to become financially sound again. When Castro was a rising power in Cuba, just prior to pushing Batista aside, he wrote to Nick, offering him a position in charge of all Cuban gambling. Monetary terms were not discussed, but it was assumed the salary would be a healthy one.

The Greek refused. It was a polite turndown. Those who

knew him guessed it was for his usual reasons: he would be unable to operate as a free-lance gambler, and he would be tied down to a job.

In Beverly Hills he had been introduced and recommended to Dr. Morris Wilburne, a specialist in cardiology and internal medicine. The pair had instant rapport and a mutual respect and admiration for one another. They engaged in many lengthy and intelligent discussions at the doctor's home. Gambling was not included in the various topics touched upon, for the doctor's knowledge in this area was limited. He enjoyed Nick's company and considered him a man of letters.

Once when Dr. Wilburne was visiting Las Vegas, and staying at the Sands with his wife, Shirley, and daughters Barbara, Harriet, and Corinne, the family had a date to meet Nick for breakfast in the old Garden Room, since renamed the Regency Room. On their way in they spotted Nick at a dice table, holding a fistful of hundred-dollar bills. He saw them and called, "I'll be with you shortly."

While they were scanning the menu, Nick made a conspicuous entrance, his arms loaded with three huge stuffed animals —a dog, a duck, a donkey. He presented them to the children, who were overjoyed. They dined leisurely, and Dr. Wilburne tried making conversation with Nick. It was difficult. Something was bothering him. He seemed preoccupied and frequently glanced at a small boy sitting with his parents at an adjoining table. The boy's eyes were glued to the stuffed animals Nick had given to the girls.

Excusing himself, Nick left the table. Minutes later he returned, carrying an enormous teddy bear, which he presented to the youngster. Now Nick underwent a metamorphosis, his mood shifting until he glowed with the pleasure that accompanies the spirit of giving.

He said he was going back to the dice table to play for a while. The doctor knew "a while" might well mean days. He asked him how he had done before breakfast.

"Dropped sixteen thousand," he said laconically.

Nick had oceans of compassion. He was continually ushering people into Dr. Wilburne's office who couldn't afford medical care. He was such a gentleman, and the situations were so justified that it didn't bother the Beverly Hills physician. It was kept within the limits of reason. Nick had a genuine sympathy for those sufferers, and brought them to the doctor out of the goodness of his heart.

His specialty was Las Vegas showgirls. One he escorted had a laceration from a car accident, a facial injury that left a scar. Dr. Wilburne referred her to a plastic surgeon. Nick took care of the expenses. Another time he appeared with a dancer who had a long, ugly scar on her right leg. Again he paid the costs of a plastic surgeon.

And there were many others.

Dr. Wilburne remarked, "You are doing a magnificent thing, Nick."

He shrugged off the compliment with a quotation: " 'Each young and beautiful being shapes around it events that are themselves young, beautiful, and happy.' "

He was asked what that was from.

"*Pélléas and Mélisande*, by Maurice Maeterlinck, Act four, Scene two, written in 1892," he recited mechanically.

During one of his trips to Las Vegas, Nick had a minor heart attack while nibbling on a chicken sandwich in a hotel dining room. He called for a telephone, which was plugged in at the table. When Dr. Wilburne came on the line Nick explained the symptoms. The doctor contacted the house physician, who ministered to Nick. A day later the Greek was playing faro.

Dr. Wilburne had asked that the hotel physician hospitalize Nick, but the gambler refused. He disliked hospitals intensely. "I'm a fatalist," he maintained, "and being in a hospital is no guarantee against death. Anyway, a hospital room is too quiet a place to die."

This attack and subsequent ones were diagnosed as attacks of congestive heart failure in which his lungs would become waterlogged. Over a period of the next ten years the attacks became more numerous, and he was on a relentless downhill course of deterioration.

He furiously fought the coming of old age. He seized Dr. Wilburne by the lapels of his coat and quoted Nietzsche: "The sick man is a parasite of society. In certain cases it is indecent to go on living. To continue to vegetate in a state of cowardly dependence upon doctors and special treatments, once the meaning of life . . . the right to life, has been lost, ought to be regarded with the greatest contempt by society."

He released the doctor from his grip. Staring at him, he demanded, "Does this apply to me?"

"Decidedly not," Dr. Wilburne told him. "You are too filled with *joie de vivre*."

Nick did not show his age. He could easily have passed for ten to twelve years younger. His thick jet-black hair still predominated over the gray streaks. The slight shoulder sag—or "stoop," as he preferred to call it, which he claimed came from standing over so many dice tables—grew more pronounced. Gamblers called it "table bent." His eyes underwent little metamorphosis. They were clear, his vision sharp.

His reflexes, though, were slowing. And he knew it.

"It takes the famous," he said, meaning himself, in a conversation with Dr. Wilburne, "longer to admit they have become old. They are sustained by memories and flashbacks of triumphs that rekindle the dying fires within, whereas those who have led dull lives have little to fall back upon for sustenance."

People's memories of Nick are kaleidoscopic, some dimming with the passing of the months. However, one in particular is unfading. The setting for it was the Sands Hotel near the cashier's box on a busy, noisy weekend, at the height of the evening. A medley of sounds filled the air: The metallic cacophony from dozens of slot machines, the chortles of joy, the groans of frustration from the players.

And there in the midst of the bedlam stood Nick, clad in a handsomely tailored powder blue suit, costly Swiss shoes, synchronizing the waving of a cigar with the meter of Rudyard Kipling's poetry, passages of which he was reciting to Dr. Wilburne.

He had learned that the doctor had taken a college course in Kipling, poet, novelist, story writer, who in 1907 was England's first Nobel Prize winner. This is what triggered his quotings.

It was incredible how this man, despite the surrounding distractions, went on and on, accurately spouting reams and reams of Kipling. His repertoire included "Departmental Ditties," "Barrack-Room Ballads," "Mandalay," "Gunga Din," and "Recessional."

His voice projected loud and clear, easily heard over the machines that were disgorging coins stuffed in by traumatized men and women. Imitative of a Greek thespian, Nick waved his arms, acting out bits of each poem, performing a most incongruous feat in a most unlikely setting, against a frenzied background of excitement, greed, personal gain.

All of which led an unknown man to mutter, shake his head, and say to no one in particular, "Nicholas Andrea Dandolos is the anomaly of the century."

During his eighty-second year, in his futile fight to hold back onrushing time, he began romancing a twenty-two-year-old showgirl who was out of work in Las Vegas. He squired her everywhere. At the conclusion of an evening of dinner and some light gambling, the couple bedded down in Nick's hotel room. The aged Greek made love with astonishing skill and vigor, causing her to sincerely pant out the cliché, "You're still the greatest."

Nick's ego rose. He pushed aside Father Time and—at least

momentarily—swept away the cobwebs of antiquity, feeling like a young man from Crete.

His return to youth was brief. The following morning, after breakfasting in the room, the girl bathed, dressed, kissed him good-bye, and said that she would see him that evening.

The gambler dressed slowly. He was experiencing difficulty breathing, and was perspiring heavily. Staggering to his feet, he walked unsteadily to the swimming pool and practically fell into a chair. He sat there for perhaps an hour, barely moving except to place a nitroglycerin tablet under his tongue to dissolve. When at length he stood up, he felt better. Fearful of a follow-up attack, he planed to Los Angeles and taxied to Beverly Hills to Dr. Wilburne's office.

"You look terrible," the doctor observed.

Nick related what had happened.

"No wonder," Dr. Wilburne said disapprovingly, and reminded him, "You're eighty-two years old, you know. What are you trying to prove?"

Nick shuddered slightly at the mention of his age and glanced around to make sure the nurse hadn't heard. While the doctor began to examine him, he said, "I proved one point, Morris, that you can use in one of your medical papers."

Dr. Wilburne asked what that might be.

"I proved conclusively that sexual drive and performance are not drastically reduced by aging."

From the age of eighty-two until he passed away two years later, Nick slowed down from his former frenzied pace. His trips to Las Vegas grew more infrequent and his hours became more regulated. He still retired late, after first eating a bite in Nibbler's Restaurant, a half-block from his hotel. Back in his room he would either watch television or read until perhaps 2:00 or 3:00 A.M., and then get into bed. His favorite author was Nikos Kazantzakis, a Greek writer and statesman. Nick particularly enjoyed reading and rereading *The Odyssey, A*

Modern Sequel, in which the author used the further adventures of Odysseus to examine the world view of Jesus, Buddha, Lenin, Nietzsche, and others. Americans were familiar with him mostly from the motion picture version of his novel *Zorba the Greek.*

Nick still didn't own a watch, but where once he cared little what hour of the day it might be, he would now periodically pick up the telephone and ask the switchboard operator. "The natural reaction of a man on whom the sands of time are running out," he explained.

As his supply of money ran lower and lower, his high standards of honesty began slowly to dissipate. Each afternoon he had a routine. He would walk from his hotel to the local office of the Sands Hotel and then cross the street to the local office of Caesar's Palace of Las Vegas for a visit with Charley Reznick and Sonny Barry. And then perhaps taxi to the law office of T. Basil Lambrose, where he continually threatened suits he failed to carry out.

On the way to these habitual ports o' call, he stopped everyone he knew along Wilshire, trying to make a touch. It was pathetic to see the former King of the Casinos—a man who had gone through five hundred million dollars—reduced to such circumstances.

Dozens of persons were still alive to whom he had handed—with no strings attached—thousands of dollars, either to give them a stake, pay off their debts, underwrite an education, or finance them in business. Few helped him. Some who felt a tinge of guilt handed him small amounts such as fifty or a hundred dollars to kiss him off and rid themselves of the Greek forever.

Harry Goldenberg and a few others were kinder. Goldenberg advanced Nick over $2,800. But a salaried man couldn't keep up this generosity forever, and Nick had to seek other sources. His success was infinitesimal. Many of his friends

whose younger eyes had sight superior to his would, upon seeing him shuffling down Wilshire Boulevard, hastily cross the
street or dodge into a building entrance.

At his wits' end, he became increasingly unscrupulous.

Two motion picture producers bought and paid him for ex-
clusive rights to his life story, and with each he signed a film
contract to receive advances of many thousands of dollars.

He also sold his betting secret systems to several publishers,
but later admitted to a friend that he was ashamed . . . that it
was the trickery of Hermes (an Olympian god with much
cunning).

"There are no winning systems," he declared. "Not even
the solar system is guaranteed to work in the face of atom
bombs."

He made many worthless promises. To justify himself he
quoted from Nietzsche, who wrote, on aging, "One must have
a good memory to be able to keep the promises one makes."
And Nick added, "My memory is getting faulty."

The last time Nick played poker was at the Monterey Club
in Gardena. A little old lady showed him the hand he hadn't
called. She had bluffed him out of the pot.

He stood up and said, "Goodnight . . . it's time I quit."

He really meant "quit forever."

On December 14, 1966, the Beverly Crest Hotel manager
and I found him naked and semiconscious on the floor of his
room. A chill wind was blowing through an open window.
He had been recuperating from pneumonia. Dr. Wilburne
was called, and Nick was rushed to Mt. Sinai Hospital in Beverly Hills.

The odds were heavy against his recovery.

A few days later he began internal hemorrhaging caused by
complications of pneumonia and a heart attack suffered after
he entered the hospital. Dr. Wilburne placed him in the intensive care unit.

Barely a week before, he had discussed death with the Beverly Hills physician. "He was unafraid of it," the doctor recalled. "Although he didn't believe in a heaven or hell, he had a strong belief in a God that controlled collectively the destinies of mankind. Nick Dandolos was a wonderful, kind man who lived to the hilt in a world of excitement that he himself created.

"His definition of death was, 'A sound sleep undisturbed by foolish dreams.' "

He died on Christmas night after receiving over sixty pints of blood, some of it donated by St. Sophia Greek Orthodox Cathedral.

The roulette wheel of life had stopped spinning.

Ironically enough, Nick died the day before Santa Anita opened for the winter horse racing season. Had health permitted, he would have been among the crowd.

Nicholas Andrea Dandolos, who had won and lost enormous fortunes during his gambling span of life, died dead broke at the age of eighty-four, the last of the big-stakes highrollers.

Anonymous donors footed the bill for hospital expenses totaling $6,600, plus funeral services here and in Las Vegas, and interment in the city he loved. The contributors, it was believed, were Las Vegas hotel and club owners, a newspaper publisher, and a scattering of friends with varied business interests.

A Greek Orthodox trisagion service was conducted for Nick at the Edwards Brothers Colonial Mortuary, Los Angeles.

A heterogeneous group of people filed before the body lying in an open casket. Among them were businessmen and women, housewives, members of the movie colony, writers, a *Life* reporter and photographer, oldtimers whom Nick had once befriended, gamblers, and bookmakers.

Most of the saddened assemblage, with the exception of the gamblers and bookmakers, signed the guest book containing a memorial record of those present. Immediately following the service, the body was placed in a gold Cadillac funeral coach and transported to the gaming capital of the nation, Las Vegas.

The funeral, on December 30, 1966, was a front page story in the *Las Vegas Sun,* whose publisher, Hank Greenspun, delivered the following eulogy:

In discussing with good friends of Nicholas Dandolos who should be the person to discuss Nick's contribution to life at his death, Benny Binion told me a story of a former governor of Texas who was attending the burial of a good friend.

The preacher finished the services and the governor stood up, walked to the front and said: "Wait a minute, you're not talking about the fellow I knew."

It isn't my purpose to usurp Father Adams' prerogatives because he isn't doing right by the fellow I knew; for indeed, the good Father has given spiritual comfort to all of us who mourn and has paid glowing tribute to Nicholas Andrea Dandolos the Man.

I come to talk about Nick the Greek . . . the Gambler.

I come to praise Nick . . . not to bury him . . . for if we are to confine Nick to the cold fastness of the grave without justifying the life he led, we would then acknowledge a misspent existence . . . a useless life lying before us in his casket.

And if we cannot support the course this man chose to follow and for what he stood, then how can any of us walk from this temple of worship and hold our heads up . . . because much of what he stands for lives in all of us and in our way of life.

More than any single person, Nick the Greek epitomized Las Vegas, the gambling capital of the world . . . for he was known universally as the "King of the Gamblers" . . . a course he set for himself purposefully, willingly and without apology.

Nick, in his early years, decided to play the game of life challengingly and daringly and he played it to the hilt. And it was not the winning that counted, but the tempting of fate . . . a fate that all men face in different forms.

And it is how fate is faced that counts . . . for those who confront their "Moments of Truth" with grace and dignity are the heroes to most of us, because we live vicariously and see ourselves cast in the role that most of us cannot play in person.

All life is a gamble and most of us are natural gamblers because we have within us the quality which makes us willing to risk our own comfort, security and present happiness for a result that seems more worthwhile.

We stake our present position against a rosier, more secure future . . . and that's what Nick did.

The major difference is that he sought a quicker decision than most of us are willing to risk. He was a man of boundless energy . . . as much as any human ever had, and he had to do something with it.

His mind was quicker . . . more agile and as exact as the most sophisticated of present-day computers . . . so he was driven to demand a quick decision, while most of us are content to wait, sometimes for a whole lifetime, for an answer.

There are many legends that have sprung up about this man, some related by friends and others . . . less glowing . . . by those whom he might have bested in the profession he chose.

Nick was a man who chose to walk a path leading down a chasm with mountains looming on either side . . . one representing evil, sinister forces and the other of royalty and kingly estates.

And as he walked, so walks Las Vegas along the straight path untainted by forces that will corrupt us and immune to the lures of noble promises incapable of fulfillment . . . but believing that all who wish to do so should enjoy the tempting of fate in whatever form one desires.

There are those who look upon gambling and gamblers as inherently evil . . . but they fail to consider that chance is part of the human equation and that taking risks is a distinct human quality.

Because . . . if taking risks in life is evil, then indeed this nation was built on such premise.

"Betcha Million" Gates was a gambler who built railroads, while some of the country's greatest fortunes were amassed gambling on the fluctuations of Wall Street . . . fortunes which later went toward the building of universities, hospitals, libraries, cultural centers, churches and places for kids . . . without hope . . . to develop physically, mentally, and become contributing members of society.

The oil fields of the country were discovered by men who gambled for oil leases and found their greatest adventure in sinking their winnings into holes in the ground that often brought disappointment, but also produced the black gold that turned the wheels of industry to make of our nation the mightiest in the world.

And even today many of the men engaged in the gaming industry here . . . gamble their money that the earth holds riches far beyond man's wildest dreams.

The leaders of the American Revolution expressly staked their lives, their fortunes and their sacred honor in signing the Declaration of Independence. They were noble gamblers, working for the welfare of their fellows.

And perhaps . . . it too can be said of Nick the Greek . . . that he worked for the welfare of his fellows.

I recall a game in 1947 at the Flamingo in which Nick pitted his daring against another Las Vegas gambler, Gus Greenbaum, in a game of Barbudi, making bets of five thousand and ten thousand on the roll of the dice.

Nick was out over a hundred and twelve thousand when he was approached for a touch by a local character who swore he'd pay the money back.

Without glancing, Nick handed him a wad of hundred dollar bills and when I asked if he ever expected to get paid back, he replied:

"I was paid back when I gave it to him."

What Nick meant was that whether you are a gambler or a ditch digger . . . one pays one's dues in this life and Nick was passing on a kindness that someone had extended to him.

With such a philosophy of life, can we say that he was less noble than the gamblers who built the railroads . . . drilled the oil wells . . . and caused universities to rise with the proceeds of their daring.

For much of the proceeds of Nick's gaming went for medical, law and business degrees for young people who needed his helping hand up the ladder . . . many of whom became successful in different parts of the world.

In Greece, South America, the United States are recipients of his munificence . . . young students he helped who are now making great contributions to society and who later repaid him manyfold when he needed to make good on some of his principal payments.

The world often wondered where Nick the Greek got his money. This was the principal source of his strength . . . the bread he had cast upon the waters.

Nick the Greek gambled because he loved it . . . it was his life . . . his constant companion . . . his need.

His was not a desire for future greatness. He thrilled to the excitement . . . the exhilaration . . . his enjoyment was in the gamble itself, and he could walk away with thousands in his pockets, or not one penny . . . and he accepted it with graciousness, dignity and philosophically.

Society judges gambling as a human weakness, but still the great industries of the nation have been built by the gamblers in Wall Street and those who daily wager the insurance companies of America that they will die before their allotted time.

When a man like Nick the Greek, who was a generous giver as well as taker, a courtly, well-educated, kindly man, devoted much of the proceeds of his gambling to constructive purposes, can we say it was a weakness or a typical human quality which motivated him?

How do we know that gambling isn't the true spirit of adventure . . . if the pioneers of this country who were the greatest gamblers gambled with oil leases, railroads . . . but nevertheless integrated into our orderly society and built its most enduring landmarks?

Who decides when a quality in man becomes a weakness in man? Which of us are capable of making such a judgment?

And if the noble gamblers who built the nation and if a man like Nick the Greek can make the transition between gambling and an orderly and useful life . . . why can't Las Vegas meld much of the good and a little of the bad, if necessary, into a useful, constructive society?

If, by its very nature, gambling makes a society, an economy or a state corrupt, then let each lawmaker, each state and each nation look to its own beginnings and into its own soul before casting the first stone.

Nick would have wanted these words spoken, for this was his thinking, his beliefs, and the only justification for his stay on earth.

Nick, more than any man, epitomized Las Vegas.

In searching for the epitome of Nick's life, my mind turned to the grand singer of songs, the great bard of strong men, Rudyard Kipling, who drew the hallmarks of greatness in his poem "If" when he wrote these words:

> If you can make one heap
>   of all your winnings,
> And risk it on one turn of
>   pitch-and-toss
> And lose and start again
>   at your beginnings . . .
> Then you're a man, my son.

And by this standard Las Vegas salutes you, Nick the Greek, a legend in your own time . . . a man.

Nick's challenge of the fates is now at an end.

His rest is eternal.

Our farewell is prideful for we knew him well.

Summoned by the single peal of an altar bell, 210 people crowded into the bandbox-sized St. John the Baptist Greek Orthodox Church at Twelfth and Carson Avenue in Vegas to pay final respects to Nicholas Andrea "Nick the Greek" Dandolos, the blueblood of the green felt jungle.

It was a funeral befitting a monarch—and that's what he was: a majestic ruler of the far-flung empire of gambling, who was often referred to as "The Aristotle of the Don't Pass Line."

The church seats were promptly filled, and over half a hundred mourners were forced to stand along the walls at the rear. Nick would have been pleased. He loved crowds.

It was a forty-five-minute service conducted by Father James Adams, who spoke in the native tongue of Nick the Greek.

The priest and psalmist chanted the Epistle readings from Chapter four, verses thirteen through eighteen, from St. Paul's letter to the Thessalonians. The gospel reading was from St. John, Chapter five, verses twenty-four through thirty.

The spoken words of Christ, the Beatitudes, were chanted. The priest also offered a prayer of absolution, and closed with the benediction.

Among the celebrities attending the funeral was entertainer Ed Sullivan.

Pallbearers were Kirk Kerkorian, Dr. Morris Wilburne, Jim Harakas, Benny Binion, Hank Greenspun, and T. Basil Lambrose.

Honorary pallbearers were Governor-elect Paul Laxalt, Governor Grant Sawyer, Mayor Oran Gragson, Sheriff Ralph Lamb, Clark County Commission Chairman William Briare, Ben Goffstein, Dick Donovan, Maurice Fitzgerald, Johnny Johnson, Viv Vickery, Moe Dalitz, Morris Kleinman, C. J. Jones, John Drew, Jack Entratter, Carl Cohen, General Charles Baron, Joe Rosenburg, Nate Schlaiffer, Jake Newman, Buck Blaine, Tom Callahan, Ed Levinson, Eddie Torres, Jack Binion, Ted Binion, Jackie Gaughan, Mel Exber, Charles King, Don Ashworth, Boy Ayou, Sundown Wells, Jimmy Snyder, Eddie Moss, Johnny Hughes, Sid Osburn, Joe Bernstein, Nate Lennett, Major Riddle, Sid Wyman, Charles Rich, Al Cahlan, Lieutenant Governor-elect Ed Fike, and Danny Stein.

Two FBI men were observed on the fringe of the gathering.

Nicholas Andrea Dandolos, the likes of whom the world may never see again, was buried in a simple plot in Woodlawn Cemetery, close to the casinos and clubs he frequented.